SAIS
PAPERS
IN INTERNATIONAL AFFAIRS

The Evolution of American Strategic Doctrine

D0061184

WESTVIEW PRESS / FOREIGN POLICY INSTITUTE
SCHOOL OF ADVANCED INTERNATIONAL STUDIES
THE JOHNS HOPKINS UNIVERSITY

SAIS PAPERS

IN INTERNATIONAL AFFAIRS   NUMBER 4

The Evolution of American Strategic Doctrine

Paul H. Nitze and the Soviet Challenge

Steven L. Rearden

The Security Studies Program

WESTVIEW PRESS / BOULDER AND LONDON
WITH THE FOREIGN POLICY INSTITUTE
SCHOOL OF ADVANCED INTERNATIONAL STUDIES
THE JOHNS HOPKINS UNIVERSITY

The drawing on the front cover represents Vauban's "first system"-a city fortification-developed in seventeenth-century France.

A Westview Press / Foreign Policy Institute Edition

Copyright © 1984 by The Johns Hopkins Foreign Policy Institute, School of Advanced International Studies

Published in 1984 in the United States of America by
Westview Press, Inc.
5500 Central Avenue
Boulder, Colorado 80301
Frederick A. Praeger, Publisher

Library of Congress Catalog Card Number: 84-51608
ISBN 0-86531-898-0

Composition for this book by The William Byrd Press, Richmond, Virginia, for The Johns Hopkins Foreign Policy Institute, SAIS

Printed and bound in the United States of America
10   9   8   7   6   5   4   3   2   1

The Johns Hopkins Foreign Policy Institute (FPI) was founded in 1980 and serves as the research center for the School of Advanced International Studies (SAIS) in Washington, D.C. The FPI is a meeting place for SAIS faculty members and students, as well as for government analysts, policymakers, diplomats, journalists, business leaders, and other specialists in international affairs. In addition to conducting research on various policy-related international issues, the FPI sponsors conferences, seminars, and roundtables.

The FPI's research activities are often carried on in conjunction with SAIS's regional and functional programs dealing with American foreign policy, Latin America and the Caribbean Basin, Africa, the Middle East, the Soviet Union, U.S.-Japan relations, Canada, security studies, international energy, the Far East, Europe, and international economics.

FPI publications include the *SAIS Review*, a biannual journal of foreign affairs, which is edited by SAIS students, and SAIS Papers in International Affairs, a monograph series which is copublished with Westview Press in Boulder, Colorado. For additional information regarding FPI publications, write to: Managing Editor, FPI Publications Program, School of Advanced International Studies, The Johns Hopkins University, 1740 Massachusetts Avenue, N.W. Washington, D.C. 20036.

ABOUT THE BOOK AND AUTHOR

This book provides a comprehensive analysis of Paul H. Nitze's influence on the making of U.S. national security policy, as well as his recent involvement in arms control negotiations. After World War II, Nitze played a major role in drafting a policy paper for the National Security Council—NSC 68—that profoundly affected U.S. strategic policy. With the outbreak of the Korean War and increased Soviet expansionism in the 1950s, Nitze and his colleagues argued forcefully for a strong program of American rearmament and an expanded peacetime defense force. Dr. Rearden brings the retrospective up to date with a discussion of Nitze's role in the SALT and Euromissile talks.

Steven L. Rearden is a member of the historical staff of the Office of the Secretary of Defense. Specializing in defense and national security matters, he is the author of *The Formative Years, 1947–1950*. He has taught at Harvard University and Boston College, and from 1974 to 1976 served as a consultant to the Office of the Secretary of Defense on U.S.-Soviet strategic arms competition.

CONTENTS

FOREWORD

THE STUDY THAT FOLLOWS is the first in a series on national security affairs. Unlike other "mainstream" monographs on strategic studies, this series will attempt to stretch the topical focus beyond the trendy. We want to treat issues and questions whose importance needs to be underscored. It is therefore appropriate to begin with an essay on Paul Nitze. Of those who have made U.S. strategic policy since 1945, the figures thus far blessed with historical badge have either held highest office or have most successfully promoted themselves with the boosting of "activist" historians. Paul Nitze has yet to be properly assessed.

Steve Rearden's analysis is unusual for three reasons. First, it shows Nitze's impact on American strategic policy far more clearly and forcefully than has been permitted by revisionist historians. Nitze's influence reached well beyond the aureole of NSC-68 and the codification of the cold war. Rearden shows that limited response, a stable nuclear balance based on rough equivalence, and deterrence through retaliation rather than preemption were all Nitze's concepts, passed on to McNamara and his successors.

Second, Rearden develops a full portraiture of Nitze's strategic thought, including the foundational values and moral concepts driving his vision. From the beginning of his influence in policy formulation to the present, Nitze placed American values and their survival in a hostile world ahead of mere technical-military solutions or definitions of "victory." From NSC-68 to his arms control efforts of today, he has sought to create a *working framework* that would avoid war, preserve

Foreword

America's physical interests, and keep Americans and their society whole as well as materially secure. His efforts to focus on conventional responses to challenge and on strategic stability are a far cry from pernicious images of him propagated by those who would make of him the ultimate cold warrior.

Finally, there is Rearden's implicit thesis on Nitze's achievements. George F. Kennan, Nitze's predecessor at State, is considered the ideocreator of "containment." Containment, based on the conviction of Soviet reform, ultimately failed in Vietnam and its aftermath. Nitze's vision, by contrast, has been the basis of American strategic policy since the 1960s. His approach to arms control through equivalence and mutual invulnerability of response is the basis for nearly all American negotiating efforts. His nonnuclear conception of limited-crisis response is now the unabridgeable norm. Finally, his notion of security through strength, in purely historical terms, has worked. As Rearden admits, the revisionists are wrong. America's military burden in the 1950s and 1960s did not result in a "national defense state." Our basic national values were never abridged, and we, as Americans, were never transformed into an evil mirror of our adversary. To have defended America without compromising it is surely an achievement.

MICHAEL VLAHOS
Codirector, Security Studies Program
School of Advanced International Studies
Washington, D.C.

INTRODUCTION

Paul Henry Nitze's public career, spanning over four decades, has placed him at or near the pinnacle of the policy process during some of the most formative and crucial moments in this country's history. A man of strong convictions, he has drawn on his experience and expertise to formulate a singular pattern of strategic thought. Yet surprisingly, Nitze has seldom enjoyed the public recognition that the record of his accomplishments would suggest he has earned. Although his recent involvement as chief U.S. negotiator at the Euromissile talks in Geneva attracted considerable press attention, it was in the end the failure of those talks that dominated the headlines. To the vast majority of Americans, Nitze's name is still unfamiliar, even though his influence and ideas have done much to shape their lives.

However history remembers Nitze, it will surely give special attention to his role in national security affairs since World War II and, in particular, his contributions in 1950 to a policy paper known as NSC 68. For a nation confused and troubled by the evident hostility of the Soviet Union, NSC 68 provided what has been termed "the first formal statement of American policy."[1] In contrast to earlier U.S. initiatives, which had generally stressed economic and political measures to block Soviet expansion, NSC 68 went a step further, urging recognition that acceptance of responsibilities abroad required an accelerated program of American rearmament lest the Soviets resort to the use of force to achieve their objectives. Nitze and others who worked on NSC 68 realized they were recommending an unprecedented departure from previ-

1

ous U.S. policy, for never before had the United States maintained a large defense establishment in peacetime. But with the outbreak of the Korean War in the summer of 1950, they felt their fears and predictions of aggressive Soviet behavior largely confirmed. As the source of basic policy, the principles on which NSC 68 were drafted have been in effect ever since.

For Nitze, NSC 68 marked the midpoint of a career that had already produced remarkable achievements and rewards.[2] He was born on January 16, 1907, in Amherst, Massachusetts, raised in Chicago, and educated at Hotchkiss and Harvard. Like many of his generation, he viewed a career in business as the proper route to success and in 1929, a year out of college, joined the investment banking firm of Dillon, Read and Company, where he acquired a reputation as a Wall Street prodigy in the middle of the Great Depression. Though inclined toward isolationism at the time of the German invasion of Poland in 1939, he sensed that American involvement in the war was unavoidable. In the summer of 1940, as a favor to his friend and business associate, James Forrestal, who had just been named special assistant to President Franklin D. Roosevelt, Nitze came to Washington, serving initially as Forrestal's aide and later as a consultant on selective-service matters to the War Department.

After the Japanese attack on Pearl Harbor, Nitze knew his return to private life would be postponed indefinitely, although already he seemed to be carving out a new career in public service. At the time of the attack, he was financial director of the Office of the Coordinator of Inter-American Affairs, a job he soon left to become head of the metals and minerals branch of the Board of Economic Warfare (BEW), under Vice-President Henry A. Wallace. In 1943 the BEW was dissolved and its functions were taken over by a new organization, the Foreign Economic Administration (FEA), where Nitze headed overseas procurement. Following a quarrel with the FEA administrator, Leo Crowley, Nitze resigned and accepted an invitation in the fall of 1944 to become a director of the newly authorized United States Strategic Bombing Survey (USSBS), which was being formed at White House direction to conduct an impartial investigation of the effects of strategic bombing on Nazi Germany. "The standard of impartiality," Nitze remembered, "was that they [the members of USSBS] should know nothing about the problem at all."[3] Although the War Department supervised the study, those responsible for its contents were civilians, drawn mainly from the ranks of industry, business, and academia. In August 1945, having completed its work in Europe, USSBS moved on to conduct a similar investigation of the air war against Japan, with Nitze now serving as the project's vice-chairman, for which he later received the Medal for Merit.

It seems clear that the bombing survey was a turning point in Nitze's life, for it was his first detailed exposure to the problems of modern warfare and the devastating impact of modern military technology, especially nuclear weapons. Some who worked on the survey, such as John Kenneth Galbraith, were appalled almost beyond measure by the destruction and suffering that the air war caused on both sides, often for limited gains that had little or no effect on the war's outcome.[4] Nitze was at times no less shocked and horrified, but on the whole he found the bombing survey an exhilarating and eye-opening experience that allowed him to bring his analytical talents to bear on matters of utmost future importance to national security. In the survey's findings, he believed, could be found the origins of the postwar concept of nuclear deterrence, though this was not the problem uppermost in Nitze's mind at the time. Rather, it was the question of what to do should deterrence fail, a question he has pondered ever since. "In preparing contingency policies," he later observed in describing the survey's investigation,

we thought that, while much had changed from the pre-nuclear era, the basic principles of military strategy were not entirely laid to waste. They were deeply modified, but they still should play a major role in the development of military strategy in the nuclear era.[5]

As principal author of the bombing survey's final report on the Pacific war, Nitze was largely responsible for synthesizing the project's overall findings and recommendations. The result was a thirty-two-page document that might be viewed as the forerunner of NSC 68 and an early blueprint of Nitze's philosophy of national security. Anticipating possible future threats, the USSBS report stressed the need for effective civil defense measures, up-to-date scientific research and development, improved intelligence capabilities to avoid a repetition of the Pearl Harbor disaster, unified direction and control of the armed forces, and last but not least, the maintenance of a peacetime defense establishment of increased size and readiness to deter any would-be attacker.[6] Of the organizational reforms the report advocated, such as unification, most soon were enacted into law by Congress as part of the National Security Act of 1947; but it was not until 1950 that Congress and the administration gave serious consideration to the general strengthening of the nation's defenses that the USSBS report had warned would be necessary.

With his bombing-survey experience and his wartime background in international finance and economics, Nitze was uniquely prepared to enter the postwar era of "national security policy," which saw an increasing tendency to blur traditionally accepted distinctions between foreign affairs and military policy. Sustained by independent means, he embarked in 1946 upon a new career in the State Department, where over the next several years he played a prominent part in setting up the Marshall Plan and the Mutual Defense Assistance Program, two key elements in the Truman administration's effort to contain Soviet expansion. After Dean Acheson became secretary of state in 1949, Nitze acquired additional reponsibilities as the department's principal liaison with the defense establishment and, subsequently, as director of State's highly influential Policy Planning Staff, in which capacity he oversaw the drafting of NSC 68.

What follows is an attempt to explore the significance of NSC 68 from the standpoint of its origins and its impact on the United States and America's role in world affairs. In the process, I hope also to shed some new light on Nitze's contributions and on the effect his ideas and influence have had on the postwar evolution of U.S. basic national security policy, including his current preoccupation—arms control.

Throughout the ensuing discussion, several themes emerge. First, NSC 68 was more than a change of policy—it was a change in the American way of life. It asserted, in the name of national security, a prior claim on scarce economic and social resources where traditionally domestic needs and interests had predominated. Second, it ushered in a more active role for the United States in world affairs, a role dependent upon the continuous maintenance of sizable military forces. Although the results, contrary to the claims made by some, have fallen short of a "militarized" foreign policy, there still has been an increased awareness of and reliance upon military power since 1950 to an extent previously unfamiliar in the American experience. In particular, the strategic balance, as reflected in the growth of large U.S. and Soviet arsenals of nuclear weapons, demonstrates most clearly the potential consequences of the unconstrained use of force, making it also the most sensitive indicator of the long-term factors addressed by NSC 68.

I would like to thank Ambassador Paul H. Nitze, Charles Burton Marshall, Ann M. Smith, and Stanley F. Smith for their helpful comments on an earlier draft of this essay. To Michael Vlahos, who suggested that I write this paper, and to Kristen E. Carpenter, whose editorial skills vastly improved this study, I am likewise grateful. Once again, I am indebted to my wife, Pamela, for her moral support. Needless to say, though I will anyway, I assume full responsibility for all matters of interpretation and any errors of fact that may appear.

1.
NSC 68: POLICY AND STRATEGY FOR THE COLD WAR

IF THERE IS ONE ACCOMPLISHMENT in Paul H. Nitze's long career that ranks above all others, it is probably his leading role in the drafting and implementation of NSC 68 during his tenure as director of the State Department's Policy Planning Staff in the early 1950s. In a sense it is the reputation of NSC 68 rather than the paper itself or what it actually said that has had the most profound, enduring impact. Existence of the report and its general contents were "leaked" to the press shortly after it was written, but it was not until 1975 that it was finally declassified and released to the public. Shrouded in the mists of official secrecy for so many years, NSC 68 had ample time to develop a powerful mystique.

There is no doubt that NSC 68 is a document of seminal importance in the post–World War II evolution of basic American security policy. Some regard it as the essential blueprint of the Truman administration's cold war military buildup, while others go so far as to say it was a clarion call for the United States to assume the role of global policeman. That its impact was profound is generally agreed. But for Nitze, the basic principles of the document remain for the most part as valid today as they were when the report was drafted more than thirty years ago.

In NSC 68 the need for and use of power—military power in particular—are of fundamental importance to the successful pursuit of foreign policy objectives and the protection of national interests. That relationship, in Nitze's view, has been axiomatic throughout history and is therefore unlikely to change. It is not a concept that coexists easily or comfortably with the more traditional American concept of foreign

7

policy normally identified with Wilson's idealism or FDR's "one world-ism." But in the aftermath of World War II there seemed less chance than ever of reshaping the world in the traditional American image of a global community working harmoniously together. In retrospect, it is clear that the basic change in official thinking occurred around 1947. By then, the accepted assumption in Washington was that the Soviet Union operated on a set of values diametrically opposed to those of the United States, and that those values, if extended to dominate the actions of other countries, would create a world environment prejudicial to the survival of the American system. What NSC 68 endeavored to supply was an overall statement of goals and methods through which power could be brought to bear on existing and future world conditions to the benefit of the United States and its friends and allies. In effect, NSC 68 signaled the eclipse of idealism and the acceptance of a new code of behavior that would deeply intensify American interest and involvement in events abroad.

The Nuclear Dilemma

The story of how NSC 68 came to be written is now well known. Early in September 1949 an air force intelligence plane flying a routine mission off the coast of Alaska picked up air samples that were found to contain radioactive debris—the first evidence that the Soviet Union had successfully detonated a nuclear device. This discovery, followed shortly by the establishment of the People's Republic of China, led to growing pressure within the administration and from Congress for a full-scale reassessment of U.S. national security policy. When President Truman approved accelerated research and development of the hydrogen bomb in January 1950, he simultaneously ordered a study of the likely future of U.S.-Soviet relations. Nitze, who had just succeeded George Kennan as director of the State Department's Policy Planning Staff, served as head of the ad hoc State-Defense policy review group that was formed to conduct the investigation.[1]

Even before the review group got down to business, Nitze had formulated tentative views on the subject. During the debate over the hydrogen bomb, the question of what role nuclear weapons should play in American defense policy had arisen repeatedly, and numerous discussions were held to explore the relationship between nuclear and conventional forces. "Those involved," Nitze recalled,

> were Dean Acheson, George Kennan, Robert Oppenheimer, and myself. Secretary of State Acheson discussed with Kennan and me what should be done in the light of the new situation. . . . Acheson made the point that, over time, the Soviets were bound to narrow America's technological lead in the nuclear field. The margin of American nuclear superiority would tend to become less and less significant as the years went by. Therefore, the United States and its allies should address themselves to restoring the conventional military balance. I felt that it would be extremely difficult in time and effort to restore the conventional military balance in Europe—the geography and the political climate were against us—and that the United States therefore should try to preserve nuclear superiority as long as possible while concurrently working on righting the conventional balance. George Kennan found nuclear weapons to be evil, but he also disliked large-scale conventional forces. He thought that the answer was to be found in greater diplomatic skill.[2]

Here in a nutshell were the diverse strains of thought that had recurred regularly in policy debates since World War II. All involved in these debates tended to agree that the Soviet Union's apparent goal of expanding its territorial and political influence posed a serious menace to the security and welfare of Western civilization. By 1947 the continuing analysis of how the United States should respond had yielded a consensus in support of a policy that Kennan described in his celebrated "X" article as one of effectively "containing" the Soviet Union's expansionist designs.[3] Disagreement most often arose over the means the United States should employ to achieve this objective. The recent advent of nuclear weapons made consensus on the question of means difficult to achieve.

Prior to NSC 68, existing differences of opinion coalesced around two competing schools of thought—one identified with Secretary of Defense James Forrestal and the other with Secretary of State George C. Marshall, Acheson's immediate predecessor and former army chief of staff in World War II.[4] In Forrestal's view, deteriorating relations with the Soviets demanded a strong military posture and greater preparedness to guard against the possibility of an armed confrontation. Although he saw no need for all-out rearmament, Forrestal felt that the credibility of the country's foreign policy depended heavily upon the credibility of its military posture. To underscore his point, he often drew the parallel of Britain and France in the 1930s, with their ill-fated attempts, made without the power to resist, to appease Hitler's Germany. By 1947 postwar demobilization had sapped the strength of America's armed forces, and it fell upon Forrestal, as the first secretary of defense, to find some way of revitalizing their effectiveness. At the time, the United States still possessed a nuclear monopoly which, combined with other favorable factors, seemed to Forrestal to give the United States "years of opportunity" during which to increase the level of its military readiness to match that of the Soviet Union. "As long as we can out-produce the world, can control the sea and can strike inland with the atomic bomb," he argued, "we can assume certain risks otherwise unacceptable in an effort to restore world trade, to restore the balance of power—military power—and to eliminate some of the conditions that breed war."[5]

Marshall, on the other hand, tended to shun calls for a military buildup in favor of concentrating on the problems of European recovery. His goal was to restore some semblance of the pre–World War II balance of power, the traditional guarantor of American security. Marshall did not doubt that the Soviet military threat was substantial, but he considered it secondary, as did Kennan, to combating Europe's postwar political and social disarray, which afforded ample opportunity for the Soviets to make inroads without recourse to arms. Like Forrestal, Marshall found lessons in the past, although the incidents that weighed most heavily on his mind and the conclusions he drew were somewhat different from those of the defense secretary. Remembering his army experience in the 1920s and 1930s—a period of resurgent isolationism and minuscule military budgets—he assumed that the American people eventually would tire of overseas involvements, seek a return to a quasi-isolationist foreign policy, and insist upon reducing military spending. It followed in Marshall's thinking that rebuilding and rearming Europe should have first priority so as to reestablish a forward line of defense, and that the task should be self-liquidating in as short a time as possible in order to avoid adverse repercussions at home.

Despite continuing tensions between Washington and Moscow, Truman's thinking fell in line with Marshall's. As much as anything, it was the cost of rearming that dissuaded Truman from beginning a military buildup. This is not to say that Truman or even Marshall found no need for military preparedness. On the contrary, Truman consistently stressed the importance of military readiness, and his defense budgets in the late 1940s far surpassed those of any of his peacetime predecessors.

Nevertheless, he felt it imprudent to burden the country with heavy military expenditures that might stifle the economy. Faced with an unprecedented rate of postwar inflation and a public debt swollen by spending on World War II, Truman decided early in his presidency that balancing the budget should be among his foremost concerns. Shortly after the war he adopted a balanced-budget policy based on the so-called remainder method that gave priority to domestic obligations and non-military foreign policy programs like the European Recovery Plan. Once these were deducted from expected federal revenues, the defense budget became whatever was left over. In practical terms, this meant annual outlays for defense on the order of $10 to $15 billion.

Because Forrestal and the Joint Chiefs of Staff (JCS) could not persuade Truman to approve requests for more money, they had to look elsewhere to offset apparent deficiencies in military capabilities. Ultimately, they came to see increased reliance on nuclear weapons and strategic bombing as the only answer. Not everyone in the military agreed that this was a satisfactory or effective solution. Uncertainty in the navy, which resented air force control of the strategic nuclear bombing mission, was especially strong; to be sure, even Forrestal had doubts. Yet at the time it seemed the only viable option, and, furthermore, it readily appealed to an economy-minded Congress.

Exactly how and when the change in military thinking took place are difficult to pinpoint, but by the end of 1948 it was clear that U.S. reliance on nuclear weapons was increasing at a rapid pace and would continue to do so barring some unforeseen occurrence. Two developments suggest the trend. First, the Atomic Energy Commission (AEC) demonstrated during the SANDSTONE tests—held earlier that year—that it could mass-produce atomic weapons by using the "levitation technique," which required less fissionable material than had been used in earlier nuclear weapons. Although the AEC tried to downplay the significance of the SANDSTONE results and advised the military not to expect any dramatic overnight improvements in the weapons program, it was clear that a major breakthrough had been achieved. Shortly after the SANDSTONE experiments were confirmed, the Joint Chiefs proposed—and the president later approved—an expansion of atomic-energy production facilities to take advantage of improved methods for recovering uranium ore. The days of atomic scarcity were near an end. With the imminent availability of more weapons came the possibility of

more diversified uses, expanded target lists, and a more formidable retaliatory capability than ever before.

The second development revealed clearly the decisive impact of
budgetary constraints in shaping the force posture. Despite a personal
appeal from Forrestal for additional funding (chiefly to avoid cutbacks
in the army and navy), Truman in early December 1948 approved a
military budget request that conformed to his previously set ceiling of
$14.4 billion for the upcoming fiscal year (FY 1950). Convinced that the
president's budget would not provide sufficient support for conventional
capabilities, Forrestal indicated he would look to strategic air power to
take up the slack. Later that same month, with Forrestal's concurrence,
the air force convened a board of senior officers who promptly recommended cancelation of several light- and medium-bomber programs; the
savings would be used to accelerate procurement of long-range (intercontinental) B-36 bombers with atomic-delivery capability. Tightened
budgetary constraints generated increasing pressure to maximize the use
of resources, with a growing concentration of assets in waging air-atomic
warfare.

None of these developments went unnoticed at the White House,
although in responding to them Truman evinced mixed emotions. On
the one hand, at no time during his presidency did he ever reject a proposal to expand the production of fissionable materials for nuclear weapons. His support of a vigorous weapons-development program was
unwavering, constituting one of the few programs he exempted from detailed scrutiny by the Bureau of the Budget. Yet on numerous occasions
Truman appeared to have serious second thoughts—even worries—that
he might be making a mistake. At one point in 1948, still hopeful that
international control of atomic energy might be possible, he urged the
Joint Chiefs to develop an emergency war plan that relied on conventional forces alone, but the project was dropped when Forrestal and the
JCS agreed that such a plan would be prohibitively expensive. Having
been the first and only president to authorize the use of atomic weapons, Truman shuddered at the thought of ever using them again, although in September 1948 he confirmed privately to his military advisors that he would do so "if necessary." Subsequently, in a public statement, Truman reconfirmed his position. That policy has survived essentially intact to the present day, but what it means is no clearer now
than it was when Truman announced it.

Because of the tremendously high stakes involved and the obvious hazards of being precommitted to a certain course of action, it is probably best that questions about the use of nuclear weapons never be answered too rigidly or definitively. Yet in Acheson's mind and in Nitze's, such questions went to the heart of conducting foreign policy. If the need for power is axiomatic, it is also axiomatic that that power be usable. And if doubt about using it exists, there will be doubts about the faithful and effective implementation of foreign policy. In short, Acheson and Nitze saw the country's defense posture becoming increasingly less flexible—a situation that was bound to reduce their options in the international arena.

Acheson's Worries

Acheson became secretary of state on January 21, 1949. He was soon to become convinced of two things: that he did not have the kind of military support he needed to conduct a fully successful foreign policy, and that he needed new advisors and assistants who would work closely with the defense establishment in developing that support. Within a year after taking office Acheson had largely solved his staffing problem and was calling for a full reassessment of basic national security policy.

According to Nitze's retrospective account, Acheson's thinking had come full circle by 1949. Having once believed that the wartime East-West coalition could be preserved, he now doubted that a satisfactory modus vivendi with the Soviets could ever be reached. Beginning with the 1946 Azerbaijan crisis, Acheson's doubts had steadily intensified. "Prior to the crisis," Nitze explained,

Dean Acheson was one of the greatest supporters of the maintenance of the wartime alliance. At that time he became disillusioned with it, not so much over Iran but as a result of the Russian refusal to consider modifying the Supreme Allied Agreement with respect to Japan. It was stated in that Supreme Allied Agreement that the Allies agreed to fix very low levels of industry in Japan. For instance, one provision was that Japan should not be permitted more than three million tons of steel production per annum, and that all Japanese steel mills in excess of that capacity were to be dismantled and the machinery turned over as reparations, primarily to the USSR and to some degree to China, Here we were, carrying the occupation burden amounting to hundreds of millions of dollars a year, with no hope of getting Japan on her feet or reducing those occupation costs unless there was a higher level of industry in Japan, which would require more steel production. But we couldn't get the Russians to agree to that. It was at that point that Acheson began to think there was really a problem here which had to be addressed. The Greek-Turkish incident the next year confirmed his view.[6]

Like Marshall, Acheson viewed the security of Europe as a matter of top priority, but he lacked confidence in existing American capabilities to hold the Soviets at bay. This did not mean that Acheson regarded a Soviet attack on Western Europe as imminent or even inevitable, although he did feel that with growing U.S. obligations, symbolized by the signing of the North Atlantic Treaty in April 1949, the question of defending Europe had to be addressed more seriously than it had been in the past. As time went on, he reasoned, a defense posture resting largely on all-out nuclear retaliation would become an extremely risky venture that would steadily lose credibility once the Soviets acquired atomic weapons of their own. That day came nearly three years earlier than most intelligence reports had predicted, with the discovery in September 1949 that the Soviets had detonated an atomic device. In Acheson's estimation, this clearly crippled the argument that nuclear deterrence could be preserved indefinitely. As Nitze later explained it, "Acheson believed that American nuclear weapons were unlikely to stop the Russians if they had once embarked upon an invasion of Western Europe; in his judgment, even attacks upon the Russian homeland would not stop such an attack."[7]

Of the personnel changes Acheson made, none more clearly revealed the direction of his thinking than his appointment of Nitze to replace Kennan as head of the Policy Planning Staff. Although Kennan had once been a favorite of Forrestal's, sometimes acting as his personal advisor on Soviet matters, he had never established the close working-level contacts in the Pentagon that Acheson deemed essential. When Forrestal stepped down as secretary of defense in March 1949, Kennan effectively lost his entrée to the defense establishment. With his usefulness thus diminished, Kennan's move to another job became virtually certain. Acheson decided that the State Department—the Policy Planning Staff in particular—needed new blood, and in the summer of 1949 he selected the man he had once characterized as "a Wall Street operator" to be Kennan's deputy and designated successor.[8]

As different in their thinking as Kennan and Nitze later became, their views at the time still flowed in essentially the same direction. Except in the area of Latin American affairs, Nitze believed their thinking ran along similar lines and noted that their respective positions on issues usually came out much the same.[9] On matters of basic policy, Nitze deferred to Kennan's lead. In drafting NSC 68, for example, he and his colleagues on the policy review group drew heavily on a policy paper (NSC 20/4) that Kennan had masterminded a little over a year earlier. This document reaffirmed the essential tenets of containment and urged the development of "a level of military readiness which can be maintained as long as necessary as a deterrent to Soviet aggression."[10] Even so, it is true that Kennan did not attach the same degree of importance as did Nitze to the role of military power in foreign policy. It is said that Kennan believed two well-trained divisions of marines were all the military power the United States needed to block Soviet expansion.[11]

In his memoirs, Kennan attributed his fall from grace chiefly to a personality conflict with Acheson, adding that as a career foreign service officer he apparently did not enjoy Acheson's full trust.[12] There may be something to this, for Acheson had served in the department before and had not been overly impressed by what he had seen. As Acheson brought more non–foreign service people like Nitze into high-level advisory posts, he gradually alienated the department's careerists, especially Soviet affairs specialists such as Kennan and Charles Bohlen, who felt that they alone possessed the necessary credentials and background for analyzing the subtle nuances of Soviet behavior. Later, when they were virtually excluded from the preparation of NSC 68, their worst fears were confirmed and, not surprisingly, they dismissed the paper's treatment of Soviet policy as crude and uninformed.[13]

Though disturbing to the department's veterans, Acheson's changes succeeded in accomplishing several significant objectives. Perhaps most important, they increased the State Department's ability to assess problems from a wide range of viewpoints, thereby enlarging its voice in policy formulation. Second, they improved cohesion within the department itself. Kennan, believing that the purpose of the Policy Planning Staff was to develop long-range projections, had not felt it necessary to maintain close day-to-day contacts with the department's desk officers. In Nitze's view, Kennan's ivory-tower approach defied the whole purpose of the Planning Staff's job, so he promptly set out to bring current and future planning closer together. In the process, much of the central staff work of coordinating policy tended to gravitate to the Policy Planning Staff, making it the focal point of contacts inside and outside the department.

As deputy director of Policy Planning, Nitze's first major assignment was to improve liaison with strategic planners in the Defense Department, a task that even an "operator" like Nitze found continually frustrating as long as Forrestal's successor, Louis Johnson, ruled the Pentagon.[14] While Acheson sought to broaden State-Defense contacts, Johnson sought to narrow them by requiring subordinates to conduct whatever business they might have with State through his office. Many of Johnson's prohibitions were impossible to enforce and some were simply ignored as a matter of necessity. But their overall effect was to create an atmosphere of severely strained relations that fueled press speculation of an Acheson-Johnson feud. Acheson eventually concluded that Johnson must have been "mentally ill." "His conduct," he insisted in his memoirs, "became too outrageous to be explained by mere cussedness. It did not surprise me when some years later he underwent a brain operation."[15]

In fairness to Johnson, the situation at the Pentagon was virtually unprecedented; his iron-fisted methods reflected his desperation to maintain control. Many of his troubles, to be sure, he made for himself, but others—intense interservice rivalry for funds, debate over competing weapons-systems, and brooding anxieties, especially in the navy, over the ultimate effects of unification—he inherited from Forrestal, who had struggled in vain to establish cooperation among the services. At the same time, Truman was more determined than ever to hold down military expenditures. In 1949, fearing a business recession that would cut federal revenues, he lowered the defense budget ceiling to $13 billion. By all accounts politically ambitious, Johnson launched a slashing economy drive to meet the president's target, apparently hoping to curry public and congressional favor and win credit that would someday propel him into the White House. Indicating that strategic air forces would now become the nation's first and foremost line of defense, he ordered cancelation of the navy's much-prized program to develop a new generation of supercarriers and, as a further money-saving move, cut the personnel strength of the army and navy by 100,000.

As Johnson accelerated the tempo of his campaign to save money, his economy program stirred increasing criticism, finally prompting the

House Armed Services Committee late in the summer of 1949 to undertake an investigation into allegations of graft and corruption in the B-
36 bomber procurement program and into Johnson's controversial decision to scrap the supercarrier. Navy witnesses called before the committee used the occasion to lobby for revival of the supercarrier. They
roundly condemned both the B-36—symbol of Johnson's defense policies—and the increased emphasis on strategic bombing with nuclear
weapons at the expense of conventional forces. Johnson escaped charges
of personal wrongdoing in the awarding of B-36 contracts, and his supercarrier decision withstood the navy's challenge, but by the end of the
investigation his authority and prestige appeared shaken.

Although it is unknown how closely, if at all, Acheson followed
the B-36 hearings, it seems clear that by the time they were over, his
skepticism of Johnson's defense policies had deepened appreciably. In
addition to the testimony of Navy critics, Acheson had access to other
information that weakened Johnson's credibility. This included a highly
classified study (WSEG R-1) that seriously questioned whether offensive
strategic air operations could be carried out successfully against the Soviet Union on the scale called for in existing emergency war plans. Prepared by the Weapons Systems Evaluation Group (WSEG), a joint technical advisory body to the Joint Chiefs, WSEG R-1 marked the culmination of a year-long behind-the-scenes attempt by the JCS to determine the effectiveness of strategic bombing. When substantially complete, the study was presented to the JCS on January 19, 1950, and then
to Truman, Acheson, Johnson, and other key officials at the White
House on January 23. Emphasizing the selection of targets likely to be
heavily defended and logistical difficulties that would impede operations, the report estimated a bomber attrition rate (somewhere between
30 and 50 percent of the attacking aircraft) that could spell disaster for
the entire offensive.[16]

Because Nitze did not attend the WSEG presentation and could not
recall, in a recent interview, if Acheson debriefed him on the meeting,
it is difficult to say with certainty whether the report's findings influ-
enced the subsequent development of NSC 68. Although NSC 68 did not
address the problems of strategy and war plans per se, it delved deeply
into the question of nuclear weapons, taking up where WSEG R-1 left
off, and recommended increased air procurement and weapons production to improve atomic strike capabilities. To this extent, the two reports dovetailed neatly, suggesting that someone on the policy review

group was aware of the defects uncovered in the WSEG study. In any case, the report could have done nothing to allay Acheson's worries over the condition of the armed forces and Johnson's defense policies. With the culmination of the H-bomb debate shortly after the WSEG briefing, matters came to a head.

In discussing the H-bomb project with Nitze, AEC Chairman David E. Lilienthal had earlier expressed deep reservations about developing the bomb without some idea of the effect it might have on the overall international situation and the future of U.S.-Soviet relations. Lilienthal deemed the bomb morally objectionable and, like Kennan, feared the growing emphasis on nuclear weapons. Nitze concurred that there were legitimate grounds, including moral ones, for concern, but he disagreed with Lilienthal's contention that the H-bomb should be shelved until its full implications could be ascertained. He felt it preferable, in view of the possibility that the Soviets might already be at work on a fusion bomb, that the United States launch the H-bomb project concurrently with a review of basic national security policy. "The upshot of this," he found, "was to satisfy Lilienthal's basic argument."[17] Likewise, it gave Acheson the opportunity he had long been seeking to try to overturn some of Johnson's defense policies.

Johnson did not feel that a review of basic national security policy was necessary, but he went along with the idea rather than delay any further a decision on the bomb. Had he known what Acheson had in mind, he might have been well advised to hold out for a better deal. Heretofore, defense policy (including the preparation of military budgets) and foreign policy had been formulated separately, linked loosely through the coordinating mechanism of the National Security Council but remaining essentially distinct entities. What Acheson sought was a fully integrated combination of the two. As David S. McLellan notes: "No one had ever successfully tackled the problem of coordinating American strategy and diplomacy. Until Acheson came along no one cared or dared to examine the political significance and risk involved in permitting the military budget to be determined in such an arbitrary way."[18] By the time Johnson realized what Acheson intended, the State Department's invasion of his turf had gone too far to be turned back.

The Threat Assessed

In approving development of the H-bomb on January 31, 1950, Truman at the same time signed a letter directing the secretaries of state and defense "to undertake a re-examination of our objectives in peace and war and of the effect of these objectives on our strategic plans, in the light of the probable fission bomb capability and possible thermo-nuclear bomb capability of the Soviet Union."[19] Nitze and the other members of the policy review group formed to conduct the study realized that to do justice to the immense problems involved, they should interpret their instructions loosely. The resulting report, probably much broader than Truman had expected, would serve as the basic guide for similar papers generated over the next decade. According to Nitze, this in itself was perhaps NSC 68's most significant contribution. "The papers up to that date," he explained, "dealt largely with the major components of policy rather than policy as a whole. . . . I think the important thing about the paper was the comprehensiveness of the approach rather than the particular recommendations contained therein."[20]

Just how the report was drafted may be summarized quickly. It was a cooperative effort, written mainly by members of State's Policy Planning Staff, with Nitze spearheading the effort and acting as chairman of the group. Armed with the president's letter, Nitze could now insist upon information and cooperation from the Pentagon to a degree that had not been possible since Johnson's advent. Contributions from the Defense Department to the study came principally from the Joint Chiefs through their representative, Maj. Gen. Truman H. Landon, USAF. Initially, Landon presented modest proposals to correct minor deficiencies in the existing force structure, but he soon became persuaded, as Nitze put it, that "we were serious about doing a basic strategic review and not just writing some papers which would help people promote special projects of one kind or another." Given the change in Landon's outlook, Nitze concluded that "there was, in fact, a revolt from within" the Pentagon against Johnson's policies, especially his emphasis on economy over preparedness.[21]

After proceeding through several drafts requiring nearly two months of work, Nitze felt the time had come for Acheson and Johnson to meet to examine the review group's progress. This meeting, held on March 22, 1950, at the State Department, nearly killed the project.

Although Nitze had kept Acheson advised with regular briefings, John-son apparently knew little of what had been going on. When he ar-rived, he cut short Nitze's oral briefing, denounced the State Depart-ment for numerous past discourtesies, and declared that he would take no position until he had time to read the review group's papers in de-tail. Acheson took Johnson aside, but their inability to hold a civil dis-cussion led to the collapse of the meeting. Johnson stalked out and Ach-eson relayed word of the impasse to the White House. "Within the hour," he later wrote, "the president telephoned me, expressing his out-rage and telling me to carry on exactly as we had been doing."[22]

From this point on, Johnson's influence within the administration declined rapidly as his differences with Acheson became more pro-nounced. While Johnson was out of town a week later attending a meet-ing of the NATO defense ministers at The Hague, the review group cir-culated its report and slipped a copy to Truman. The Joint Chiefs and service secretaries uniformly supported its recommendations. Faced with the choice of concurring or of offering an embarrassing lone dissent, Johnson endorsed the report and urged Truman to place it before the National Security Council for further study. In April the report entered the council's serial number file as NSC 68. Finding that he could not sup-press the report, Johnson decided to accept it, though he remained skep-tical about whether it would lead to any significant change of policy.

NSC 68 begins with a dramatic comparison of the American and Soviet political systems, underscoring the inherent conflict between them and, by extension, that between East and West. The purpose of the American system, as enunciated in the preamble to the Constitu-tion, is "to assure the integrity and vitality of our free society, which is founded upon the dignity and worth of the individual." The purpose of the Soviet system, in sharp contrast, is to assure the supremacy of com-munist leaders and their "absolute power, first in the Soviet Union and second in the areas now under their control." Characterizing the Soviet Union as a "slave state" pursuing ruthless policies of oppression and ex-ploitation at home and abroad, NSC 68 depicted the world as being di-vided between two irreconcilable philosophies—one committed to the preservation of freedom, as pursued in the West, and the other com-mitted to the perpetuation of a totalitarian dictatorship bent on noth-ing less than world domination controled from Moscow. "What is new," the report argued, "what makes the continuing crisis, is the polarization of power which now inescapably confronts the slave society with the free."[23]

Critics have since tended to dismiss the opening sections of the report as mere hyperbole, designed either to capture readers' attention (Truman's in particular) or to give vent to pent-up cold war frustrations. Yet a close reading of this part of the report suggests something more than propaganda. Indeed, it suggests a redefinition of the Soviet threat as an almost permanent menace to the American way of life. Heretofore the prevailing assumption in official circles, nurtured by the optimism of Kennan's "X" article, was that containment of the Soviet Union over time would produce internal changes that would alter Soviet behavior, causing a mellowing of Soviet hostility toward the West and eventually the rise to power of new Soviet leaders who would be less antagonistic, less paranoid, and less bent on expansion. NSC 68 holds out no such hope, or little at best. It views the Soviet Union as an implacable foe whose internal political system is self-perpetuating and whose dangerous policies and philosophy are therefore likely to threaten the West for many years to come, and perhaps indefinitely. Instead of being a temporary phenomenon as depicted by Kennan, the cold war as viewed in NSC 68 had become the more or less permanent state of U.S.-Soviet relations. It might ease up from time to time, or it might intensify, but it would not go away, even under the pressures brought to bear on the Soviets by continuing American containment.

The report then goes on to survey the strengths and weaknesses of the Soviet system. Most menacing, it felt, were the Soviet Union's military capabilities, which NSC 68 found to be "far in excess of those necessary to defend its national territory," leading to the conclusion that their only possible purpose was to support Moscow's "design for world domination." Military expenditures in the Soviet Union consumed nearly 14 percent of the gross national product, as against 6 to 7 percent in the United States. Only in atomic armaments did the United States hold a commanding lead—though as time went on this advantage was expected to diminish. Citing the most recent agreed intelligence estimate, the report predicted that by mid-1954 the Soviet Union would have a stockpile of approximately 200 atomic bombs, a number thought to be sufficient to "seriously damage" the United States. And if the Soviet Union successfully developed a thermonuclear capability, the threat would be "tremendously increased."[24]

Faced with this growing danger, the review group endeavored to assess what counteracting steps the United States could take, looking specifically at four courses of action. Two of these—a return to isolationism and the initiation of a preventive war—the report dismissed as impractical and inadvisable because the role of the United States was to provide world leadership and to forestall wars, not start them. A third option—to pursue a continuation of current policies—seemed no less ill-advised. "From the military point of view," NSC 68 argued, "the actual and potential capabilities of the United States, given a continuation of current and projected programs, will become less and less effective as a war deterrent." This left the fourth option, the only one the report found realistic and prudent—"a substantial and rapid building-up of strength in the free world . . . to support a firm policy intended to check and roll back the Kremlin's drive for world domination."[25]

To retain a credible deterrent and to prepare for any possible future emergency, the report urged the United States to step up nuclear weapons production and "increase as rapidly as possible our general air, ground and sea strength and that of our allies to a point where we are militarily not so heavily dependent on atomic weapons." At a minimum, the United States should have forces in being or readily available to defend the Western Hemisphere, protect the mobilization base at home, conduct offensive operations on a scale "sufficient to destroy vital elements of the Soviet war-making capacity," defend lines of communication, and provide aid to allies. Additionally, and as part of a "comprehensive and decisive program," the report endorsed the development of "an adequate political and economic framework for the achievement of our long-range objectives," a "substantial increase" in American military expenditures, an enlarged program of foreign military assistance, some increases in foreign economic aid, intensification of intelligence activities and covert operations, and stronger measures for internal security and civil defense.[26]

The need for these measures followed logically from what the policy review group perceived as the principal source of danger—"a strong surprise blow" similar to the Japanese attack on Pearl Harbor in 1941. The warning implicit in NSC 68 was that the United States could ill-afford another Pearl Harbor disaster, least of all one mounted by an enemy using nuclear weapons. The purpose of rearming, therefore, was not merely to deter the Soviets from launching an attack, but to be able to absorb the first strike if it should come and to have sufficient conventional and nuclear forces survive to respond effectively. Hence the call for a peacetime buildup that would reduce the need for protracted mobilization in wartime and assure the successful conduct of military operations until the enemy capitulated or reinforcements could become available.[27]

What becomes clear from this line of reasoning is that while the authors had a healthy respect for nuclear weapons, they did not view them as necessarily decisive or likely to become so. If the United States could take steps to absorb a nuclear attack, so, too, could the Soviet Union. A surprise nuclear attack would indeed be devastating, but it need not determine the final outcome if the necessary preparatory steps were taken and there were sufficient dispersed and survivable forces in being. In Nitze's view, such skepticism about the effects of nuclear weapons derived initially from the findings of the U.S. Strategic Bombing Survey and was reinforced by the limited size of the nuclear stockpiles then in existence. The conclusion to be drawn, Nitze thought, was that nuclear war need not spell total disaster or annihilation, but should be avoided by all possible measures.

Here Nitze's influence appears especially to have exerted itself. Of those who served on the NSC 68 policy review group, Nitze had more personal firsthand experience with the effects of nuclear weapons. As vice-chairman of the USSBS in 1945, he was among the earliest to inspect Hiroshima and Nagasaki. Although the USSBS investigation confirmed the awesome destructive power of the atomic bomb, it also turned up some surprising findings that left Nitze skeptical: in Hiroshima rail traffic had resumed forty-eight hours after the attack; tunnel shelters in Nagasaki had provided effective protection from the attack, even at ground zero; nonradioactive vegetation was soon growing again immediately under the centers of the explosions; and factories on the periphery of the cities were virtually undamaged, out of operation only for lack of raw materials.[28] "Frankly," Nitze later recalled, "the emotional effect of seeing what had happened at Darmstadt was greater, in a surprising way, than it was at Hiroshima and Nagasaki."[29]

But in the final analysis it was not a military confrontation with the Soviets that the authors most feared. Rather, it was the prospect that over time there might occur a weakening of "the integrity and vitality of our system" brought on by a progressive erosion of values or a deteriorating willingness to defend them. "Even if there were no Soviet Union," the report argued, "we would [still] face the great problem of the free society, accentuated manyfold in this industrial age, of reconciling order, security, the need for participation, with the requirements of freedom."[30] In other words, the defense of freedom was a constant, ongoing battle. That it now involved the Soviet Union—a country of immense and growing military capabilities—did not in any way alter the nature of the struggle, although it did necessitate a redoubling of American awareness and effort. Increased military power was of primary importance because it represented the most visible demonstration of will, a signal to Moscow that the United States would go to any length to protect its freedom.

The essence of NSC 68 was its all-encompassing recommendation of "a rapid and sustained buildup of the political, economic, and military strength of the free world."[31] The key word is *sustained,* which implied the need for a sharp departure from all previous assumptions governing the development of national policy. Chiefly, this meant rejecting Marshall's assumption that the American people would not tolerate open-ended foreign commitments or heavy defense expenditures year after year. During the preparation of the report, the members of the policy review group held lengthy discussions about whether the program they envisioned could be sustained and whether the American people had the will to pursue it. The members were certain that the United States could mobilize the necessary resources, but there was considerable doubt as to the willingness of the American people to bear the burdens for an indefinite time and to make the sacrifices entailed by such an effort. Marshall's response, had he been asked to comment, would probably have been "no." The review group, perhaps knowing what it was likely to hear, apparently made no attempt to solicit Marshall's advice, although it did consult others, including former under secretary of state Robert Lovett, J. Robert Oppenheimer, James B. Conant, Ernest O. Lawrence, Henry D. Smyth, and Chester I. Barnard of the Rockefeller Foundation. All tended to agree that public acceptance of the program could not be taken for granted and, as Barnard put it, that "the government was going to need assistance in getting public support for the national effort which would be called for."[32]

Initially, however, it was President Truman's acceptance rather than the public's that the policy review group needed. One way of doing this was to delete financial estimates from the report, thereby leaving the president free of any binding prior commitments should he choose to approve the report for implementation. Privately, Nitze and others who worked on NSC 68 estimated the cost at between $35 and $50 billion annually over the next several years, but Nitze made his personal estimate known only to Secretary Acheson, and there is no evidence that Acheson relayed this information to the president. Given Truman's tough-minded approach to money matters, it followed logically that if he could be persuaded that the danger was as great as it seemed, requiring all the sacrifices that were deemed necessary, so too could most other people. The report conceded that the program it outlined would be "costly," and it recommended higher taxes to avoid deficit budgets, but it simply did not belabor these points.

There is, of course, much in NSC 68 that has become the object of continuing criticism. Its rhetoric, for one thing, strikes some readers today as exceptionally harsh and tough, more so, at any rate, than would seem necessary for a document labeled "top secret" and therefore unlikely to attain wide circulation—unless, perhaps, the authors had some other purpose in mind for the paper. Nitze insists that the report was meant solely for internal consumption, and as for the style: "We wrote it that way for clarity."[33] Nonetheless, in striving for clarity, the paper tends toward oversimplification, giving East-West relations in particular the aura of a black-and-white struggle. The idea that there was in fact a clear dichotomy in the world between a "slave" society in the East and a "free" society in the West could be misleading because very few countries outside the Soviet bloc were "free" by American standards of democracy. Many, especially in Asia and Africa, remained colonial holdings from the days of European imperialism, while in Latin America right-wing, authoritarian regimes abounded. Moreover, communism was by no means the monolith that NSC 68 portrayed it to be. Yugoslavia's defection had already taken place and Acheson was counting on a similar occurrence in China to thwart the extension of Soviet influence in the Far East. Yet the picture of communism in NSC 68 is that of a galvanized movement, directed from Moscow and virtually impervious to any accommodation with the West.

Perhaps the most curious part of the report was its treatment of nuclear weapons. Even though it urged substantial increases in conventional forces, NSC 68 still regarded nuclear weapons as crucial to American security and likely to remain so as the Soviets expanded their atomic arsenal. This implied that the more weapons the Soviets stockpiled, the more the United States should stockpile—a classic action/reaction phenomenon. Where this process might lead or be expected to end, the report did not say, although it seemed to suggest that both sides eventually would acquire offsetting nuclear capabilities. Until that point was reached, however, the report cast doubt on the probability that U.S. reliance on nuclear weapons would significantly diminish. Acheson wanted a better balance between conventional and nuclear forces, but he could not have been overly reassured that such a balance would soon be achieved.

Yet for all its faults, real and alleged, NSC 68 is still a remarkable document, distinctly representative of the troubled, uncertain times in which it was written. An emotional but still analytical paper, it addressed an issue that was without precedent in American experience—the rise of an adversary with seemingly limitless ambitions, committed to an ideology that claimed the tide of history was on its side, and willing to allocate tremendous resources to carry out those ambitions. Since World War II, the searing realization of the enormity of this challenge had led the United States to rethink its role in world affairs and to undertake initiatives such as the Marshall Plan, the Greek-Turkish aid program, and NATO that earlier generations of Americans would have seen as beyond the pale of contemplation. Yet for all the effort and resources that had been expended to counter the Soviet threat, it seemed only to grow more bold and menacing. The point that NSC 68 endeavored to drive home was that there was no "quick fix" to the problem of Soviet power, no easy solution that would soon guarantee peace, prosperity, and international harmony. That a confrontation with the Soviets might quickly escalate into global nuclear war compounded the problem, making it all the more urgent for the United States to raise its guard. The American people were not accustomed to such continuous psychological exposure to these dangers; NSC 68 clearly implied that they would have to adjust, lest they risk losing the values and freedoms they held most dear.

Acceptance and Implementation

Contrary to the impression conveyed by Acheson in his memoirs, Truman did not approve NSC 68 as soon as he officially received it in April 1950.[34] In fact, his initial reaction to the report was one of typical caution. Reluctant to commit himself to any new or enlarged programs without knowing what they might cost, he directed the creation of an ad hoc interagency committee, with heavy representation by his economic advisors, to assess the report's potential budgetary impact. At the same time, Secretary of Defense Johnson ordered the Joint Chiefs to prepare itemized listings of force-level deficiencies. These studies were still in progress when the Korean War erupted on June 25, 1950. Confronted with the sudden outbreak of war and fearing an escalation of communist aggression, Truman sent U.S. combat troops into Korea and notified Congress that he would need supplemental appropriations for defense and military assistance totaling $10 billion, the first of several such requests he would make before the end of the year. Finally, on September 30, he got around to signing a memorandum (NSC 68/1) approving NSC 68 "as a statement of policy to be followed over the next four or five years."[35]

This sequence of events raises the intriguing question of what Truman would have done about NSC 68 had the Korean War not intervened. Most, including Nitze, regard the adoption of NSC 68 as a major departure of policy—the first step toward a rearmament program that would radically alter priorities at home and drastically expand the scale and scope of American commitments abroad. Even if Truman had not approved the report, however, it seems probable that the results would have been essentially the same because of the Korean conflict and the worries it generated. NSC 68 provided a new rationale that effectively subordinated all other concerns to meeting the needs of national security. Presidents tend to hedge major decisions of this sort as long as possible; and Truman, despite his celebrated pronouncement that "the buck stops here," was no exception. He took more than five months to make up his mind on the report and then acted only after events seemed to point out the course he should take.

In Nitze's view, some event would sooner or later have forced the president's hand. As early as February 1950 Nitze had expressed growing concern over signs of "a boldness that is essentially new" in Soviet behavior—an apparent willingness on the part of the Soviet Union, emboldened by its new nuclear capability, to assume risks that it had eschewed previously. Although he did not rule out the possibility of general war if the Soviets miscalculated and went too far, Nitze anticipated that they would localize their aggression in areas where the United States would be hardpressed to respond. Among the areas in which the Soviets seemed most likely to foment troubles, Nitze singled out Indochina, Berlin, Austria, the United Nations, and Korea.[36]

Nitze's assessment was essentially a visceral one. He had no solid proof of what the Soviets might be planning, nor did intelligence reports predict a general worsening of the world situation. There seemed nothing to provoke undue alarm, at least nothing that compared with the seriousness of the situation two years earlier, when the Soviets overthrew the Czech government, made menacing gestures toward Norway and Finland, and launched the Berlin blockade. At that time, the United States still had a monopoly on nuclear weapons, yet this had not stopped the Soviets from seeking to make gains and to exploit weak spots where they could. Given this perspective, it seemed to Nitze only logical that with a nuclear capability, the Soviets would feel more confident than ever and would try somehow to capitalize on their newly acquired strength.

Nitze's most disturbing "evidence" of Soviet malignity came from Alexander Sachs, an economist with Lehman Brothers. Sachs arrived at Nitze's office one day in the spring of 1950 with a set of papers warning that the Soviets saw the "correlation of forces" as having turned in their favor. Sachs believed the Soviets would act cautiously at first, probably through one of their more reliable satellites. From this he further deduced that an attack on South Korea loomed in the very near future.[37] But as accurate as Sachs's warning proved to be, it was not the first such report to cross Nitze's desk. Indeed, similar assessments had recurred regularly in official channels ever since the first signs of a North Korean military buildup appeared in 1947. In any case, Nitze doubted whether much could be done to forestall a conflict until Truman reached a decision on NSC 68.

There is strong reason to believe that even without Korea, Truman would have approved NSC 68. Withholding approval would have inflicted a terrible blow to Acheson's prestige and credibility, and by the spring of 1950 there was no question that Truman regarded Acheson as his closest, most trusted advisor. Some increases were therefore virtually assured, yet without Korea they probably would not have been on the order of magnitude Acheson clearly preferred. The longer Truman ruminated over the report, the more probable it became (as the members of the NSC 68 review group expected) that the Bureau of the Budget and others would whittle away at its recommendations until they fit within a budget that Truman thought the country could afford and the public and Congress would accept. This seems to have been what Truman himself had in mind with the instructions he issued to his budget director, Frederick J. Lawton, at a meeting on May 23. "The President indicated," Lawton noted, "that we were to continue to raise any questions that we had on this program and that it definitely was not as large in scope as some of the people seem to think."[38]

Still, any increase would have served Acheson's immediate purpose, for it would have represented the tacit repudiation of Johnson's economy program and, with that, the beginning of the end of policies predicated on economic feasibility. This in itself would have been a significant departure from past practice, but it probably would not have been enough to guarantee the continuation of a "sustained" buildup. Only with the onset of the Korean emergency did Truman accept the full range of NSC 68 recommendations as well as the thinking behind them.

As it turned out, the buildup occasioned by the Korean War left its architects less than fully satisfied with the results, though in expenditures and new programs it was indeed an impressive effort. From a prewar base of less than $13 billion in fiscal year 1950, national defense accounts soared to $48.7 billion in FY 1953, nearly a fourfold increase that consumed 13.5 percent of the gross national product, compared with 4.8 percent three years earlier.[39] At the same time, the United States poured billions more into a greatly expanded military assistance program, added new facilities to accelerate the production of tactical and strategic nuclear weapons, built a chain of overseas air bases that virtually encircled the Soviet Union and China, and strengthened its covert operations and psychological warfare capabilities. The rearmament of Germany began, NATO acquired a multinational high-command structure, and four additional divisions of American combat troops were sent to Europe. Elsewhere, the United States signed a mutual security agreement with Japan, concluded a similar arrangement with Australia and New Zealand, and assumed much of the financial burden of keeping French forces fighting communism in Indochina, while American troops did the same in Korea.

Despite a long list of accomplishments, however, the job seemed neverending; the goals often appeared within reach but were somehow unattainable. At one point late in 1950, Nitze expressed astonishment at "the enormous cost" of the buildup and the "rather small forces" it promised to yield.[40] But it was not simply the cost of rearmament that gave cause for concern; with clever budget management, a surge in the economy from defense orders, and acceptance of the need from time to time for deficit financing (eventually to become a regular part of the budget process), fiscal problems took on relatively less importance than before. Rather, it was the continuing uncertainty over the public's willingness to sustain the buildup that most worried its supporters, thus giving rise to such groups as the first bipartisan Committee on the Present Danger, which set about trying to educate the public on the need to rearm.[41] Part of the difficulty arose from the increasing unpopularity of the Korean War as it dragged on, promising no more than a bloody battlefield stalemate and seemingly fruitless negotiations with an inscrutable enemy. The outbreak of the war had elevated NSC 68 to the status of national policy; yet, ironically, the longer the war continued, the harder it became to rally a national following for that policy. As Acheson soon realized, the war diverted attention from the true danger. "We are fighting the second team," he conceded, "whereas the real enemy is the Soviet Union."[42]

The backlash came in November 1952 with the election of a new administration that promised to end the war as its first order of business. Once in office, Eisenhower went even further, reimposing curbs on military spending and reverting to defense policies that again stressed reliance on nuclear weapons—this time more heavily than ever. As Kennan had experienced three years earlier, Nitze saw his power and influence wane, as his views on national security policy grew to be more and more at odds with those of Eisenhower and his secretary of state, John Foster Dulles. Though Nitze was tentatively offered a new job in the Defense Department, the appointment never materialized owing to the opposition of conservatives in Congress who felt that Nitze was too closely identified with Acheson. As much as he disagreed with the new administration's policies, friends of his say he deeply regretted not being kept on.

If the policies of the Eisenhower administration seemed to diverge from those of the Truman period, the thinking behind them remained basically the same. During the years of the Truman buildup, "national security" acquired a new breadth of meaning that no change of administrations could easily erase. It became the focal point and ultimate justification for governmental endeavor, an all-encompassing concept that carried with it a strong claim on the country's resources. To this extent, the basic purpose of NSC 68 had been achieved. Once this point of departure was reached, there could be no turning back. As long as the Soviet threat existed, the United States had no choice but to maintain a vigilant, ever-ready posture and a high level of preparedness.

The authors of NSC 68 were well aware of the great risks involved in the course they advocated. Much human and material sacrifice obviously would be required and, indeed, the potential for abuse was enormous, especially in the area of covert and clandestine activities. Perhaps they underestimated the full and lasting impact their report would have. But at the time it seemed to them the only solution to the problem of Soviet power without recourse to a devastating world war. Whatever the future held, NSC 68 would be a part of it, the enduring statement of philosophy behind the transformation of American strategic policy.

2.
BASIC NATIONAL SECURITY POLICY SINCE NSC 68

Since NSC 68, U.S. BASIC NATIONAL security policy (BNSP) has followed a fairly fixed and predictable course, emphasizing a strong military posture with ready forces and active support abroad for resistance to Soviet expansion. In geopolitical terms, the goal has been to protect the status quo, basically as it came into being after World War II, without recourse to thermonuclear war. Despite these broad lines of continuity, however, much debate has taken place over the components that will make this strategy workable. Shifting budgetary priorities, the advent of new technologies, and continuous refinement of the basic strategic concept have all contributed to the fluid evolutionary environment. Although broad policy and objectives have remained essentially the same, the means of achieving them have undergone progressive modifications.

Nitze's uniqueness lies in his nearly uninterrupted involvement in this evolution of policy, sometimes as a critic, but more often as a high-level advisor and participant in the policy-making process. Largely excluded from official circles during the Eisenhower years, he reentered the policy arena in the 1960s to hold major posts in the Kennedy and Johnson administrations and to serve thereafter as an advisor and negotiator on arms control. But though he later held higher offices and had broader responsibilities, it is arguable that Nitze's most creative and enduring accomplishments came as director of the State Department's Policy Planning Staff in the early 1950s, when the drafting and implementation of NSC 68 took place. Never again would Nitze—or anyone else for that matter—be in such a key position to guide the development of a study that had as dramatic an impact on the nation's destiny.

Those who argue that NSC 68 was responsible for what they see as the militarization of American foreign policy since 1950 tend to overlook the inherent limitations the report cited on the use of force. While urging a strengthening of military capabilities, NSC 68 clearly questioned the advisability of surmounting our problems with the Soviet Union in all instances by military means. Significantly, it rejected the idea of preventive war at a time when America's preponderance of nuclear power might conceivably have made such an option attractive. Improving the country's military posture was not an end in itself but rather a means to facilitate the achievement of fundamental objectives, chiefly to assure the nation's survival under a nontotalitarian form of government. Diplomatic solutions, where they could be formed, were always preferable to war, but NSC 68 recognized that diplomacy, like military power, had its limits. It was the gray area between war and diplomacy where serious trouble was most likely to arise, where the choice between war or peace was uncertain. NSC 68 endeavored to bridge this gap not by making the use of force more readily available and therefore more tempting, but by establishing a closer balance between foreign policy objectives and the military programs necessary to support them.

There was, however, an even deeper function served by NSC 68. In effect, it gave the concept of national security an importance it had never before had except in wartime—a claim on resources equal to or greater than that of all competitors. The result was a new, peacetime era of higher military budgets in support of a defense establishment of unprecedented peacetime size. This constituted a sharp departure from past patterns of public policy, a dramatic postwar change that appeared unavoidable if the United States were to fulfill its chosen role as world leader and contain Soviet expansion. What cemented the new commitment to "national security" was the proliferation of nuclear weapons in the hands of both the United States and the Soviet Union, and the realization that a conflict involving such weapons would have disastrous consequences.

Of the many ingredients that have helped shape national security policy since 1950, nuclear weapons have ranked foremost in importance from the outset. Nitze found nuclear war a horrible prospect, but as the contents of NSC 68 suggest, he did not think it at all unlikely if the United States failed to maintain an adequate nuclear deterrent and likewise failed to strengthen its conventional capabilities. The Eisenhower administration chose not to follow this costly path but embarked instead upon a course aimed at deterring new conflicts by emphasizing the likelihood of their escalation into nuclear war. Such thinking did not sit well with Nitze, who during the Eisenhower years found the need for an alternative increasingly urgent.

The "New Look" of Massive Retaliation

During the eight years of the Eisenhower administration, from 1953 to 1961, the basic strategic policy of the United States reverted to the reliance on nuclear weapons that in some respects had characterized the prevailing strategy of the late 1940s. In 1949, while serving as acting chairman of the Joint Chiefs of Staff, Eisenhower had helped advance that strategy by urging Secretary of Defense Louis Johnson to make strategic bombing and air-atomic retaliation the centerpiece of defense planning. "Since we have always stressed the value of military preparation as a deterrent to war," Eisenhower advised Johnson, "it seems to me obvious . . . that we cannot and must not fail to provide a respectable long-range strategic bombing force." Faced at that time with Truman's determination to hold down military expenditures, Eisenhower concluded that "preserving and enhancing this capability" were essential to assure an adequate defense.[1]

As before the Korean War, budgetary concerns reemerged in 1953 to preoccupy the new administration. Like Truman, Eisenhower viewed a strong defense and a sound economy as the twin pillars of national security, but he faulted Truman for having jeopardized the economy by allowing the military buildup to proceed too quickly. As the first Republican president in two decades, Eisenhower had close ties to the business community, which was highly critical of the enormous growth in federal spending during the Korean War. Eisenhower resolved to meet this problem head-on, with an immediate overall budget reduction of $5 billion, with defense bearing the brunt of the cutback.

To offset any loss of strength, Eisenhower directed the Joint Chiefs and the National Security Council to look closely at the expanded application of "new weapons," a euphemism for nuclear weapons—although the term may have been meant to apply to chemical and biological weapons as well. Initially, the JCS resisted cuts in military strength, arguing that uncertainty over the use of nuclear weapons compelled them to accept the continuing need for substantial conventional forces. To get around this problem Eisenhower agreed to modify Truman's policy on use of atomic weapons and to seek new legislation that would relax strictures on the dissemination of atomic-energy information. The result, after lengthy discussion and debate, was Eisenhower's approval in October 1953 of a new basic national security policy paper (NSC 162/2) that called for development and maintenance of

1. A strong military posture, with emphasis on the capability of inflicting massive retaliatory damage by offensive striking power;
2. U.S. and allied forces in readiness to move rapidly initially to counter aggression by Soviet bloc forces and to hold vital areas and lines of communication; and
3. A mobilization base, and its protection against crippling damage, adequate to insure victory in the event of general war.

Of equal importance, it is worth noting, NSC 162/2 stressed the need for "a sound, strong and growing economy."[2]

At its principal objective—cutting and containing defense costs—the administration's policy turned out to be a qualified success. The only cuts Eisenhower actually achieved were those he made during his first two years in office. These came out of budgets inherited from Truman, whose own plans called for similar reductions at the end of the Korean War. Once the Korean "bulge" in the budget was gone, Eisenhower faced the problem of steadily rising costs owing to inflation and other pressures. These he countered largely by deferring new procurement and by stretching out approved programs. Still the largest item in the federal budget, national defense consumed an annual average of around 10 percent of GNP during Eisenhower's tenure. The president's major accomplishment lay in reducing the rate of growth of military spending. At the end of the administration's eight years in office, total obligational authority for defense was just over $44 billion, roughly the same as when Eisenhower entered the presidency.[3]

The chairman of the Joint Chiefs, Adm. Arthur W. Radford, publicly described the administration's defense policy as a "new look" in national security, a choice of words Eisenhower regretted because it seemed to imply "a far more radical change in the composition of our armed forces than was truly the case."[4] Nonetheless, there was no denying that the administration regarded conventional forces as an expensive burden and that its goal was to economize by increasing reliance on U.S. nuclear capabilities, by stepping up covert operations against unfriendly regimes (e.g., Iran and Guatemala), and by urging other noncommunist states to do more in the way of providing for their local security. One result was a headlong rush into a series of bilateral defense treaties and mutual security agreements, fashioned after NATO, with the intent of bolstering indigenous defenses in the Middle East and on the Asian periphery of the Sino-Soviet bloc.

With growing worldwide responsibilities came the problem of how to meet them. In a speech to the Council on Foreign Relations on January 12, 1954, Secretary of State Dulles dismissed the notion that new commitments abroad need entail a corresponding expansion of U.S. capabilities. Rather, the solution was to be found by "placing more reliance on deterrent power, and less dependence on local defensive power." Although local defense would still be important to contain Soviet expansion, it "must be reinforced by the further deterrent of massive retaliatory power" and by the maintenance of "a great capacity to retaliate, instantly, by means and at places of our own choosing." The net effect, Dulles argued, would be "more basic security at less cost."[5] This, in essence, was what the New Look was all about—a reordering of priorities purported to do the same job as NSC 68, but at a lower cost made possible by returning nuclear weapons to the forefront of policy. Henceforth, the New Look and "massive retaliation" would be practically synonomous.

For Nitze, Dulles's "massive retaliation" speech was the opening event in a seven-year struggle to reverse and correct what he considered the mistaken assumptions and misguided policies of the Eisenhower administration. Soon after Dulles gave his address, Nitze drafted a ten-page analysis in which he gave vent to frustrations that had been building since he left government the year before. Already suspicious of Dulles's personal integrity, Nitze deeply resented the "partisan" tone of the speech and its implication that the previous administration had squandered the nation's resources on a needless military buildup. Security through reliance on nuclear weapons was, in Nitze's view, a dangerous myth. "If we are to attain victory, or peace with justice and without defeat," he argued, "we must attain it with nonatomic means while deterring an atomic war." While conceding that such an undertaking would be expensive, Nitze flatly rejected Dulles's assertion that it was more than the economy could sustain. "It is perfectly clear," he felt, "that the problem is one of leadership and will, not of dollars and cents." Ultimately, there was bound to result a repetition of past mistakes. "In other words," Nitze found, "we are to retreat to the pre-1950 policy of focusing primarily on the risk of general war and of concentration primarily upon atomic weapons."[6]

Nitze was essentially correct that the New Look bore a close resemblance to the pre–Korean War policies of the Truman administration. But at the same time there were also important differences. For one thing, the New Look involved a much broader and more diversified application of atomic energy. In the late 1940s atomic weapons had been crude, bulky devices, so large that they required specially built delivery aircraft, and so few that their use in an emergency might have readily depleted the stockpile. Recently released official figures show that the United States had an arsenal of fifty Nagasaki-type bombs by mid-1948. Although no official figures have been declassified for the years after 1948, Bernard Brodie once offered his informed guess that the stockpile contained around 300 bombs on the eve of the Korean War. Thereafter, as the promise of the SANDSTONE experiments began to materialize and new production facilities such as the Savannah River complex came on line, the stockpile increased rapidly. According to one set of unofficial estimates, the United States had approximately 1,000 warheads and bombs by the summer of 1953 and nearly 18,000 by the end of the decade.[7]

Not only were more weapons available, but technical improvements in design and delivery systems meant they could be adapted to a more diversified range of uses. During the 1950s, as earlier, the air force had the predominant voice in strategic warfare planning—manned bombers capable of delivering high-yield nuclear and thermonuclear weapons were the mainstay of the country's deterrent force, the key to making "massive retaliation" a credible policy. But by 1953 breakthroughs in the development of lower-yield, "tactical" battlefield weapons that could be borne by fighter aircraft or fired from artillery pieces gave the army and the navy a growing role in the nuclear mission. To take full advantage of the expanding arsenal and increased diversity of delivery systems, the New Look necessitated a new set of assumptions about the role atomic weapons would play in future wars. As Secretary of Defense Charles E. Wilson once explained it, American defense "is based . . . on the use of such atomic weapons as would be militarily feasible and usable in a smaller war. . . . In other words, the smaller atomic weapons, the tactical weapons, in a sense now become the conventional weapons."[8]

There was no doubt in Eisenhower's mind that any war involving an exchange of nuclear weapons, even tactical ones, would produce untold horrors. With the advent of the atomic bomb, he believed, modern warfare had reached the point where "destruction of the enemy and suicide for ourselves" were virtually indistinguishable.[9] The only sure solution he saw over the long run was "to lighten the burdens of armaments and to lessen the likelihood of war."[10] Yet as menacing to humanity as he felt nuclear weapons to be, he was also deadly serious about employing them against an aggressor and actively encouraged the military services to develop doctrine and plans detailing their use. Nor apparently was he averse to threatening nuclear retaliation to achieve U.S. objectives. Although the evidence is still somewhat circumstantial, it points strongly to the conclusion that the president was prepared to order the use of nuclear weapons if the Chinese did not promptly end the Korean stalemate in 1953, and that he contemplated a similar course of action in 1955 and again in 1958 during the crises over Quemoy and Matsu. What is less clear is whether Eisenhower's "nuclear diplomacy" actually accounted for the settlements that were reached in these episodes.[11]

The most innovative planning for the use of nuclear weapons was that undertaken by NATO in fashioning a "new approach" to the defense of Western Europe. Modeled after the New Look, the New Approach emphasized reliance on nuclear weapons—chiefly the new battlefield "tactical" variety—to overcome NATO's presumed inferiority vis-à-vis the Soviet bloc in conventional forces. Here perhaps was Eisenhower's sharpest departure from the guidance laid down in NSC 68, which had found the maintenance of a strong conventional force, especially on the central front in Europe, almost as important as preserving a superior nuclear deterrent. Eisenhower summarily rejected such thinking. "Two more divisions or ten more divisions, on our side," he insisted, "would not make very much difference against the Soviet ground force."[12]

The resulting reassessment culminated in 1956–57 when the European members of NATO reluctantly endorsed a new U.S.-sponsored political directive and a new strategic concept paper, both of which

stressed the early and extensive employment of nuclear weapons to re-
pulse a Soviet invasion. Proponents of the New Approach, led by its
principal architect, Gen. Lauris Norstad, the supreme allied com-
mander, consistently maintained that NATO had, and would continue
to have, a powerful conventional capability to deal with a variety of
contingencies, but they also readily conceded NATO's growing dependence on its atomic arsenal.[13] In fact, the new strategic concept left
little room for a conflict limited to conventional forces, for it assumed
NATO's use of nuclear weapons from very near the outset of hostilities
and called upon the allies to plan for the defense of NATO territory as
far forward as possible, making use of nuclear weapons regardless of
whether the Soviets did so first.

Introducing nuclear weapons into Europe as the mainstay of
NATO's defenses was, from Nitze's standpoint, the ultimate folly of the
massive retaliation concept, because it dramatically and needlessly increased the risk of a nuclear confrontation. "I happen to think," he remarked, "that tactical nuclear weapons add little to our true security or
to that of Europe. It is hard to imagine circumstances in which tactical
nuclear weapons could be usefully employed in Europe unless backed up
by the use of the full power of our strategic nuclear forces."[14] This, of
course, would mean global nuclear war, which was entirely at odds with
what the administration sought to achieve. Yet having whittled down
its nonnuclear capabilities for reasons of economy, Nitze saw the United
States reduced to no other option should a major crisis erupt. Because
time to mobilize would be limited, the logical course would be a pre-
emptive first strike. "In an all-out atomic war," he maintained, "if we
do not achieve a decisive advantage in the initial blow, we will lose all
advantage from having a vastly superior industrial base."[15]

The administration's dilemma, Nitze contended, arose from a confusion of ends and means, a thesis he elaborated upon in his "Atoms,
Strategy and Policy" article published in Foreign Affairs in 1956. Here,
he drew a sharp distinction between the administration's "declaratory
policy" (massive retaliation) and the absence of an effective "action
policy" to go with it. To threaten full-scale nuclear retaliation, the
United States had to be able and, more important, had to be willing to
carry out its threat. Otherwise, any statement the administration might
make would lack credibility and hence the power to deter Soviet aggression. In Europe, U.S. determination might be firm, but what of
other regions—the Middle East and Asia—where the United States also

had commitments? At what level of aggression should we draw the line? Should a localized attack, such as happened in Korea, elicit the same response as an invasion of Europe? The greater the gulf between the declaratory policy and the action policy, Nitze believed, the greater the risk of a miscalculation by the Soviets leading to a nuclear exchange.[16]

All in all, the New Look left Nitze deeply troubled. He saw it not as the product of prudent imaginative planning but as a dressed-up relic—a throwback to outdated policies from before 1950, when the United States had been the world's only nuclear power and still relatively immune to direct Soviet aggression. That those conditions no longer existed seemed to matter little to the Eisenhower administration, which had become preoccupied with saving money and exploiting the alleged wonders of nuclear energy. Nitze, with a long career in financial matters, did not dispute the need for a sound economy; nor did he doubt that nuclear weapons had an important role to play in the nation's security. But it was a role, he felt, that needed more careful thought and definition than those currently in office appeared willing or able to give it. "If it is said, as it sometimes has been," wrote Nitze, "that we cannot afford another war like Korea, the answer is that such a war is the only kind which we or anyone else can afford. Only a madman would attempt to avoid it by plunging into the unspeakable disaster of a World War."[17]

The Gaither Report and Asilomar

Nitze's simmering discontent with Eisenhower's approach to national security finally found an effective means of expression through his participation in 1957 on the Security Resources Panel, known commonly as the Gaither Committee after its chairman, H. Rowen Gaither, a former president of the Ford Foundation who also sat on the board of directors of the RAND Corporation. The panel's original purpose was to conduct an evaluation of civil defense programs, which had been criticized in Senate hearings chaired by Lyndon Johnson in 1956 and early 1957 for being inadequate to meet the nation's needs in case of a Soviet surprise attack. In response, the Federal Civil Defense Administration devised a national shelter plan. If adopted, the plan would cost close to $40 billion to implement. Eisenhower, seeking to mute the growing controversy, resorted to a tried and true political stratagem: In

April 1957 he approved the creation of a committee of private citizens to conduct an impartial study. Initially asked to serve as a consultant to the panel, Nitze later assumed the coauthoring of its final report.[18]

Like the policy review group that had prepared NSC 68, the Gaither Committee interpreted its instructions loosely. According to one recent account, the impetus for broadening the study came largely from Albert J. Wohlstetter, a well-known RAND analyst, who insisted that civil defense was secondary to the problems of strategic air command (SAC) vulnerability. Wohlstetter, like Nitze, was dubious of the massive retaliation doctrine and had worked out calculations showing weaknesses in SAC's retaliatory capability under a Soviet attack.[19] Acting on his suggestion, Gaither sought and obtained approval to extend the panel's investigation to include the entire range of offensive and defensive weapons systems as well as the problems posed in four general areas: active defense; passive defense; social, economic, and political implications; and quantitative assessments. Intense from the beginning, the review gathered even more momentum when, in August 1957, the Soviet Union announced the first successful test flight of an intercontinental ballistic missile (ICBM). Sputnik I followed in October, a shock to the American public and a major embarrassment to the administration whose own space program had yet to get off the ground. With no operational ICBMs of its own and no proven way of defending against missile attack, the United States seemed increasingly vulnerable to a Soviet first strike capable of decimating the U.S. strategic retaliatory force, a prospect that left members of the Gaither Committee, and Nitze in particular, deeply disturbed.

Although it had been promised full cooperation, the Gaither panel apparently had little, if any, access to the most important recent intelligence, including U-2 spy plane photographs of the Soviet Union. These, as Eisenhower may have suspected, cast doubt on Soviet claims of missile superiority and showed a program later characterized by one White House advisor to be "leisurely and relaxed."[20] But even if the Gaither Committee had seen all the pictures that had been taken by 1957 (probably a very small number; overflights had begun only the previous year), it seems highly unlikely that they would have altered the panel's findings. Soviet achievements were indeed real, and they marked breakthroughs in weapons and space technology that the United States had yet to equal. The most unfortunate consequence was that by guarding the pictures so closely, Eisenhower inadvertently helped promote the very thing he wanted to avoid—the perception of an ominous and growing "missile gap," with the Soviet Union well in the lead.

In many ways—not surprisingly, in view of Nitze's involvement with committee's work—the Gaither report bore close resemblance to NSC 68. Submitted to Eisenhower in November 1957, it outlined a five-year program with a primary emphasis on deterring an attack through increased offensive capabilities and a secondary emphasis on deterrence through enhanced measures to restrict civilian casualties. In the first category, the report recommended improvements in the readiness and alert status of SAC's bombers, accelerated U.S. ICBM and IRBM missile development, an enlarged early-warning system, and an augmented conventional capability for limited war situations. In the second category, the report called for increased research and development in such areas as radars, antimissile defenses, and antisubmarine warfare, and endorsed the construction of civilian fallout shelters nationwide.[21] In other words, like NSC 68, the Gaither report saw the need for a general strengthening of U.S. defenses.

After examining the Gaither report's proposals, the Joint Chiefs noted that nearly all of the recommendations in the first category had either been approved for implementation or were being studied (technical problems were the chief obstacle to further action).* But it was not the report's proposals per se that aroused controversy. Indeed, the Gaither report's implicit philosophy was quite different from that of the Eisenhower administration. In effect, the report argued that massive retaliation was no longer a credible doctrine (if, indeed, it ever had been) because it rested on the outmoded assumption of overwhelming American nuclear superiority. Even though the United States might still be able to inflict damaging retaliatory blows against the Soviet Union (a proposition the Gaither report found open to question because of SAC's limited dispersal capabilities), the Soviets now possessed—or eventually would possess, as they had demonstrated—forces that could strike with devastating effect. The strategic nuclear balance was shifting, and as it shifted the vulnerability of the United States would increase, causing a

---

*For the Joint Chiefs' comments, see JCS 2101/284, December 4, 1957, sub: Report by the Joint Strategic Plans Committee . . . on Report to the President by the Security Resources Panel, RG 218, National Archives. The issue appears to have been one of timing, not the programs themselves. The Gaither panel wanted to accelerate the deployment schedule, while the Eisenhower administration continued to pursue, in most instances, a stretch-out policy.

corresponding rise in the need for greater protective measures, such as the shelter program, and uniformly improved military capabilities. In these circumstances, the effectiveness of American foreign policy would depend more than ever on the military strength behind it. United States forces should be able to deter the Soviets from launching a major attack on the United States and to operate successfully at a level below that of an all-out nuclear war in the event of crisis.

Here in embryonic form were the essential elements for the restructuring of forces that in the 1960s would yield the doctrine of "flexible response," with antecedents traceable directly to NSC 68. As in the 1950 paper, the Gaither report conceded that its recommendations would be costly to implement (about $19 billion for the highest-priority programs and $25 billion for those in the second category) and that these additional burdens, if accepted and approved, would undoubtedly require sacrifices in the form of higher taxes, temporary federal deficits, and cutbacks in other areas of government spending. But the committee did not feel that such sacrifices would impose undue hardship on the economy or encounter any strong public opposition. "The American people," the report contended, "have always been ready to shoulder heavy costs for their defense when convinced of their necessity."[22]

These words must have had a familiar ring to anyone who had read NSC 68. But unlike NSC 68, the Gaither report was written by a group of outsiders who were largely powerless to influence the course of policy except by pointing out what they saw as its errors and shortcomings. At a meeting of the committee and NSC members on November 7, 1957, Eisenhower wondered if the situation was as serious as the Gaither report contended. Concluding that it was not, he saw no urgent need for an overhaul of his national security policy. While terming the report "useful" in correcting certain defects and deficiencies, particularly in SAC's alert-reaction procedures, he doubted that its findings provided "a master blueprint for action" and pointed out that it "failed to take into account certain vital information and other considerations." Dulles voiced similar objections and added that he thought the report's endorsement of a costly shelter program might harm relations with the NATO allies. "If we build shelters and they cannot," he argued, "we can write off all our European allies." Moreover, he dissented from the committee's view that the economy would be able to bear the costs of the recommended programs. Eisenhower concurred. "Our security," he later reflected, "depended on a set of associated and difficult objectives:

to maintain a defense posture of unparalleled magnitude and yet to do so without a breakdown of the American economy."[23]

Though the Gaither report failed to bring about an immediate change of basic policy, it had exposed what Nitze and other critics considered serious weaknesses and defects in the nation's defense that otherwise might have gone unnoticed or unattended. Of equal importance to Nitze, the report had outlined an alternative to massive retaliation—an alternative that anyone acquainted with NSC 68 would have had little trouble recognizing.

What is especially interesting about Nitze's involvement with the Gaither report is the apparent effect it had on his perception of the strategic balance. Heretofore, Nitze had consistently asserted the need for U.S. strategic superiority. Now, with increasing frequency, he spoke of reaching a point of "equilibrium" or "stability" in a crisis that would produce a standoff in the strategic arms competition and thereby lead both sides to reassess their military options. Accordingly, the first task, in Nitze's view, was to develop a secure deterrent capable of disabusing the Soviets of the notion that the United States could be rendered defenseless by a first strike.

How this might be accomplished became the subject of Nitze's highly speculative and later controversial speech before the Asilomar National Strategy Seminar in April 1960. Following logically in the footsteps of the Gaither report, the Asilomar speech questioned the utility of a national security policy predicated on indefinitely preserving American nuclear superiority in the form of a disarming first-strike capability. But it left listeners stunned and incredulous by suggesting, even as a "grand fallacy," that the United States unilaterally scrap its more vulnerable strategic-weapons systems and consider placing SAC under a NATO command responsible to the United Nations. Nitze said he had long advocated maintaining strategic superiority, calling it a "Class A" capability which, in the event deterrence failed, could totally disarm an opponent in a first strike. A "Class B" capability, on the other hand, could absorb a first strike and retaliate with "unacceptable damage to the enemy." "If both we and the Russians succeed in building a Class A capability," he argued, "this means that neither will have a truly secure Class B capability. In other words, the value of the initiative, the initial strike, would then be conclusive. Such a situation would be highly unstable." Having reassessed the matter, Nitze now felt that the time had come for the United States to concentrate on developing a reliable Class B posture and invite the Soviet Union similarly to restrict its strategic aims. "The essential definition of a Class B capability," he added, "is that it denies a Class A capability to the other side."[24]

Asilomar was the Gaither report carried to extremes. Both recognized that the strategic balance was undergoing fundamental change and that something had to be done to assure American survival against the growing threat of Soviet nuclear power. But unlike the specific remedies in the Gaither report, Asilomar offered as a "grand fallacy" a total, all-encompassing solution based on a sweeping restructuring of America's military power. Although similar to the "assured destruction" concept that gained currency in the 1960s, it had more in common with the idea of minimal deterrence. To be effective, it would have to have given priority to damage-limiting measures designed to guarantee a reasonably high survival rate for its offensive forces. Critics were suspicious. As long as the strategic balance weighed in favor of the United States, even with the possible existence of a "missile gap," many naturally viewed the speech as a proposal to trade our strategic posture for that of the Soviet Union. Nitze, realizing the misunderstanding that his speech had caused, soon beat a hasty retreat. "Separation between a Class A and a Class B military capability should be qualified," he admitted. "Obviously, any such black-and-white distinction is wrong—there are all kinds of decisions in between. I was merely using this as a simplifying device which I thought would be useful in drawing attention to an issue worth debating."[25]

Asilomar was Nitze's first and last venture into the realm of grand fallacies. Henceforth, his thinking would revert more and more to the orthodoxy of NSC 68, with the goal of restoring America's military power—strategic as well as conventional—to a level he considered commensurate with the dangers the country faced from abroad. What Nitze saw as the Eisenhower administration's unwillingness to invest adequate resources toward these ends left him convinced that new policies and new leadership were urgently needed. With John F. Kennedy's election, Nitze and like-minded others would have the opportunity not only to have their advice heard but enacted as well.

Flexible Response in a MAD World

As with Dwight Eisenhower's election eight years earlier, the arrival of the Kennedy-Johnson administration in 1961 meant a reassessment of U.S. basic national security policy. As a senator and presidential candidate, John F. Kennedy was highly critical of the Eisenhower defense program, faulting it for allowing the country to fall behind the Soviet Union in strategic missile development and for failing to provide a viable limited-war capability. Once in office, Kennedy resolved to address these problems as well as a third—Khrushchev's threat in a speech made on January 6, 1961, to unleash a wave of communist-directed "liberation wars," or what some in the West termed "sublimited conflicts." Soon to emerge was the policy of "flexible response," tailored to provide for graduated levels of conflict in place of large-scale nuclear retaliation. "We have been driving ourselves into a corner," Kennedy said, "where the only choice is all or nothing at all, world devastation or submission—a choice that necessarily causes us to hesitate on the brink and leaves the initiative in the hands of our enemies."[26]

At the outset of his presidency, Kennedy had the benefit of a strong consensus among the public and in Congress that more was needed to bolster the nation's defenses and accelerate its young space program. The launching of Sputnik had much the same effect as the outbreak of the Korean War: It jarred the country out of complacency, providing renewed impetus for government initiatives and public sacrifice. Still reeling from the shock of Sputnik, Americans responded enthusiastically when in his inaugural address Kennedy asked them to "bear any burden, meet any hardship."[27] By the end of the decade, however, with the United States embroiled in the controversial Vietnam War, the consensus of 1961 had turned to disarray, leaving many, like Nitze, who saw a continuing need for a strong defense, uncertain of the future.

Perhaps the most influential cabinet member in the Kennedy administration (next to the president's brother, Bobby) was the hard-driving, analytically minded secretary of defense, Robert S. McNamara, former president of the Ford Motor Company. Nitze, who had been Kennedy's campaign advisor on foreign and defense matters and had headed a postelection task force on national security policy, expected to be named deputy secretary of defense, but found that McNamara preferred Roswell Gilpatric for the post. "What he wanted me to do," Nitze recalled after talking with McNamara, "was to work specifically on the matters of military policy and the interface between foreign policy and defense policy."[28] This put Nitze in the sensitive job of assistant secretary of defense for International Security Affairs (ISA), a post crucial to the development and execution of NATO programs, military assistance, and the entire range of U.S. military commitments abroad. It was therefore something of a step down for Nitze when in 1963 Kennedy persuaded him to become secretary of the navy, a job with more prestige but less influence than ISA. Finally, in 1967, he moved back into the mainstream as deputy secretary of defense, the job he had envisioned having seven years earlier.

The first few months of a new administration are usually its most formative with regard to the policies and programs it will pursue. In Kennedy's case, this period was rife with changes. Some were merely cosmetic, designed to project the image of young, forceful leadership moving the country out of the rather staid Eisenhower era. Others, however, would have a profound impact on national security policy for many years to come.

Defense received special attention. Once the uncertainty and confusion over the missile gap was settled (it did exist, but it was the Soviets who lagged), McNamara vigorously exercised the mandate given him by the White House to conduct a thorough reappraisal of strategy and capabilities. Because of the enormous investment of resources involved, the long lead-time for research and development, testing, and deployment, and faced with projections of growth in Soviet capabilities, the first item on his agenda was to accelerate development of strategic missile systems, focusing on the Polaris submarine and the silo-based Minuteman. At the same time, Kennedy formed an interagency group to look into the development of more effective forces for counterguerrilla warfare. With the Berlin crisis in the summer of 1961, attention shifted to the strengthening of conventional capabilities and the augmentation of ground and air forces in Europe, with Nitze designated to coordinate the buildup. By the end of the year, with progress reported in all three areas, flexible response seemed well launched and under way.

To support his new policy, Kennedy was compelled to seek increases in military spending that added $5 billion to the defense budget during his first year in office, this on top of additional funds to expand the space program, military assistance, and foreign aid. Thereafter, defense expenditures held steady at around $50 billion annually until escalation of the Vietnam War forced further increases in the mid-1960s. Yet even with the increases necessitated by the Kennedy buildup and Vietnam, defense claimed less of GNP than at any time since the Korean War, dropping from 9.1 percent in FY 1961 to 7.8 percent in FY 1970. Whereas Truman and Eisenhower had followed the practice of setting yearly budget ceilings, Kennedy decided that strategic objectives should govern the level of expenditures. However, he made clear that he did not intend to write the Pentagon a blank check: The watchword was cost-effectiveness. Through the introduction of sophisticated "budget-programming" procedures and "systems analysis," McNamara not only held down costs, but in the process achieved a degree of control over the military budget never before considered possible.

Although Nitze had long advocated the kind of policy Kennedy adopted, he felt that something more was needed—a blueprint, on the model of NSC 68, to establish priorities, clarify objectives, and draw defense and foreign policies into line. During the 1950s it had been routine procedure for the National Security Council to update annual statements of basic national security policy, a practice Nitze thought should continue. Shortly after taking office, he therefore directed ISA's Policy Planning Staff to draft such a paper for submission to the NSC, while at the same time a similar effort went forward in the State Department— initially under George McGhee's supervision, and later under Walt W. Rostow's. Both projects soon collapsed—according to Rostow's account, because of a dispute over the role and use of tactical nuclear weapons.[29] But as Nitze discovered also, Kennedy simply did not believe in the utility of BNSP papers—he thought they would hinder his freedom of action. As a result, the NSC system fell by the wayside, and McNamara's annual "posture statements" (the first of which was issued in 1962) became the accepted formulation of the administration's basic policy. Problems requiring coordination were dealt with through ad hoc interdepartmental committees. "His method of operation," Nitze later said of Kennedy, "did give a greater lift and imaginativeness to national security policy, but it had its failures as well as its successes in execution." Most serious of all, Nitze felt, was that staff-level coordination became "somewhat unpredictable."[30]

The absence of an overall policy blueprint may not have seemed too debilitating in the beginning. Kennedy—intelligent, energetic, and resourceful—proved an adept student of world politics. After overcoming the Bay of Pigs fiasco, the results he obtained were quite impressive: a negotiated settlement of the Laos situation; a standoff that preserved the status quo in Berlin; and, finally, the humiliating setback inflicted on the Soviets during the Cuban missile crisis. But beyond the immediate successes these episodes represented, there loomed the larger questions of where the United States should put its priorities, what it should hope to accomplish, and, ultimately, how far it was prepared to go to achieve its goals. In the failure to address these questions in a systematic, thoughtful manner may rest the explanation for the Vietnam tragedy.

During the 1950s answers to these questions came relatively easily. The overall objective was to confine the Soviets to their established orbit (Dulles's rhetoric about "liberation" notwithstanding) and to avoid military involvement in sideshows like Korea and Indochina by threatening massive nuclear destruction of the Soviet homeland should Moscow transgress the boundaries of other countries. Kennedy was equally committed to containment, but he doubted that threats of massive retaliation would prevent the Soviets or the Chinese communists from probing our defenses in areas that the United States might not feel obliged to defend with the full weight of its power. Moreover, he sought to diminish the risk of general nuclear war by reducing U.S. reliance on nuclear weapons. To do so, he accepted the idea put forth by Nitze and others of graduated deterrence, involving a "pause" or "firebreak" between conventional conflict and escalation to a larger war. "The ability to commit forces in the intermediate range of armed combat," Nitze argued, "should make more credible to the U.S.S.R. the certain prospect that we will back our nonnuclear forces by the use of our strategic nuclear capabilities should that be necessary."[31] But as appealing as this concept may have been in the United States, it often got a tepid reception abroad, especially among the NATO allies. Not only did it revive the specter of another large-scale conventional war; it would also require an investment of resources for strengthening conventional capabilities that the Europeans were loath to make. Since 1949 NATO had relied on American assurances of prompt nuclear retaliation in case of Soviet aggression. Now, it seemed, Washington was hedging and wanted to shirk its responsibilities.

To overcome European objections to a conventional buildup, Kennedy offered the enticement of a multilateral nuclear force, the ill-fated MLF. Nitze, who was partly responsible for the MLF negotiations, was skeptical that a multilateral arrangement of the sort proposed could be made to work and, in any case, he doubted that the French could be persuaded to go along. His assessment soon proved correct. The French, copying the British course in the 1950s, opted for their own nuclear arsenal, which in turn prompted the Germans, who were prohibited from having atomic weapons, to insist upon stronger assurances of nuclear support from the United States. The net effect by 1967, when NATO finally adopted a new "flexible response" strategy paper (MC 14/3), was some strengthening of conventional capabilities, offset more than ever by the proliferation of nuclear weapons across NATO Europe.

Although the Kennedy administration tried to play down the military utility of nuclear weapons, many of its members, including Nitze, were well aware that, politically, nuclear weapons had a great deal to offer. This was especially true after 1961, when it became clear that the United States continued to enjoy a strategic advantage that the Soviets were still in no position to challenge. Behind the rhetoric of flexible response there was always the implied threat of wholesale nuclear retaliation. Although some, like McGeorge Bundy and Maxwell Taylor, now contend that it had no influence on their thinking or recommendations at the time, there is little doubt that U.S. strategic superiority was a central factor in causing the Soviets to withdraw their missiles from Cuba in 1962. And while it may have played no role at all in the Laotian settlement, it was almost certainly an important part of the U.S. resolve to stand firm against the Soviets in Berlin. In other words, strategic superiority was still a valuable commodity, perhaps as integral to the practical application of the flexible-response doctrine as it had been in buttressing the Eisenhower administration's massive retaliation policy.

For Nitze, the Berlin and Cuban episodes provided convincing proof that a strong defense modeled on the principles laid down in NSC 68 was still the key to effective containment of the Soviets. Having once toyed with other ideas, he readily acknowledged his belief, reaffirmed by events in the early 1960s, that only through the maintenance of strength could the Soviets be deterred and perhaps enticed to become more cooperative. "It would seem to me to be of the utmost importance," he remarked less than a year after the Cuban crisis, "that neither we nor our allies at this point reduce our defense capabilities. It is only as the Soviets become persuaded that there are no easy gambits for them to exploit by rapid changes of tactics that we can expect to move forward to the sound negotiation of more serious issues with them."[32] For critics who dredged up his Asilomar speech, Nitze had a tough, no-nonsense response. At the Senate hearings for his confirmation as secretary of the navy in 1963, he declared:

I am a strong believer in the importance of maintaining superiority over the Communist bloc in every element of our military power. . . . I believe that only by maintaining this superiority of strategic and nonstrategic military forces can the United States have the optimum opportunity to use its military power short of war to support its foreign policy or be in a position to win a military victory, at the lowest level of conflict adequate to do the job, if war should, nonetheless, occur.[33]

Like McNamara, Nitze accorded first importance to strategic weapons, feeling more than ever after the Cuban crisis that U.S. strategic superiority was integral to the maintenance of effective deterrence. "Perhaps the most persuasive factor influencing the Soviet Union against aggressive courses of action," he observed, "is the Western nuclear arsenal."[34] But the nagging question throughout the 1960s was how long the United States could preserve its superiority in the face of growing evidence of a Soviet strategic buildup. After the Cuban missile crisis and Khrushchev's ouster in 1964, new rulers in the Kremlin made clear their determination to draw equal to the United States in strategic power. By the end of the decade they were on the verge of achieving their goal, having surpassed the United States in the number of deployed land-based ICBMs and drawing close to the United States in sea-based systems. Only in the number of strategic warheads and manned long-range bombers did the United States still hold a commanding lead.[35] Although Soviet missiles were less sophisticated and lacked the accuracy of the U.S. counterparts, it was obvious that a watershed had been reached. No longer could the Soviets be intimidated as they had been during the Cuban crisis.

Although a Soviet strategic buildup had long been forecast, its implications were nonetheless deeply disturbing, especially from the standpoint of preserving the options of flexible response. The most endangered of these was the concept of controled response, which McNamara had embraced in his 1962 Ann Arbor speech. As McNamara described it, the purpose of controled response was to reduce the potential damage of a strategic exchange, largely by concentrating on counterforce targets.

With the U.S. forces retargeted primarily on Soviet military installations rather than on Soviet industry and cities, as had been the practice in the 1950s, McNamara felt that Soviet leaders would have "the strongest imaginable incentive to refrain from striking our own cities." It followed that if military installations were to become the first targets, the United States would need a highly reliable "second strike" capability that could absorb an enemy attack and limit further damage by destroying the remainder of the Soviet strategic force before it could launch another salvo, a job that rested for the most part with the relatively invulnerable Polaris submarine fleet. Broadly speaking, what McNamara was advocating bore close resemblance to the concept of a Class B capability as outlined by Nitze in his Asilomar speech in 1960, though it differed in two important respects: First, it assumed a continuing balance of strategic power favorable to the United States; and second, it would require a somewhat larger force structure in order to accommodate a broader range of contingencies.[36]

By 1965, however, amid growing evidence of an accelerating Soviet buildup, McNamara concluded that the United States could not maintain strategic superiority forever, nor could it hope to achieve a truly effective damage-limiting strategy with the technology then available. Backing off from what he had said at Ann Arbor, he began to advocate a concept he termed "assured destruction," later rechristened "*mutual* assured destruction" (MAD) to drive home the point that both sides were equally vulnerable. Despite the introduction in the late 1970s of the "countervailing" strategy, with refined targeting options and renewed emphasis on striking Soviet military and political installations, MAD is still the key to the U.S. strategy of nuclear deterrence. Instead of limiting damage to counterforce targets, MAD projected suicidal losses for both sides in a nuclear exchange. Initially, McNamara defined assured destruction as the ability to inflict losses amounting to 25–30 percent of the Soviet population and 70 percent of Soviet industry, although he later pared these figures to 20–25 percent population fatalities and one-half of Soviet industry. Either way, however, the results conjured up the image of a return to the supposedly discredited massive retaliation doctrine. "I think we could all agree," McNamara told the Senate Armed Services Committee in 1967, "that if they [the Soviets] struck us first, we are going to target our weapons against their society and destroy 120 million of them."[37]

Whether Nitze had a better alternative in mind is difficult to tell, because Defense Department records for the 1960s remain largely closed. Being a committed "team" player, Nitze seldom aired his disagreements or misgivings over policy in public while serving in an official capacity. Judging from what he has since said and written, he accepted assured destruction as the essence of deterrence, the most formidable argument possible for Moscow not to initiate a full-scale confrontation. But he also saw it as posing significant problems should crises similar to Berlin and Cuba arise. Although assured destruction might deter, it provided virtually no meaningful political leverage for dealing with the Soviets except at the level of general nuclear war. Today he still disagrees with those who, like Henry Kissinger, question the value of strategic superiority, particularly as it might affect behavior patterns in the midst of a crisis. "The stronger side cannot be wholly confident that there would be no response," Nitze argues, "but it can act with greater confidence in such a situation. When the probable ratios are not that one-sided, even the stronger side must act with caution."[38]

One solution to the problem of growing Soviet power would have been for the United States to engage in a further strategic buildup of its own. But with the heavy and increasingly unpopular burden of Vietnam and a growing number of expensive social programs to finance, a further buildup held little appeal and would probably have encountered stiff political resistance. After assessing its other options, the Johnson administration decided to concentrate on securing arms control agreements with the Soviets to head off a costly new round of competition, while moving ahead with stopgap measures such as MIRV and the increased hardening of missile silos to strengthen existing capabilities. Buying more weapons, it seemed, would not necessarily buy more security.

For Nitze, the imminent demise of America's era of nuclear superiority meant that a workable balance of power would be more difficult to maintain than ever before. It would mean general-purpose and nuclear forces of sufficient size and effectiveness to deny the Soviet Union the chance to establish a clear-cut lead. It would also mean greater emphasis on such nonmilitary programs as civil defense. What remained to be seen was whether the American people, disillusioned by the experience of Vietnam, would rise to the challenge and accept the necessity, as Nitze saw it, of continuing to make sacrifices. In 1950, NSC 68 had charted a course that the country followed more or less faithfully for the next two decades. By the time the Johnson administration left office, the country was tired—tired of Vietnam, of steadily rising defense budgets, and of what appeared to be the growing threat of nuclear holocaust. It wanted a break from the journey and looked to détente and strategic arms talks with the Soviets to provide a pause, if not permanent respite.

3.
THE ARMS CONTROL IMBROGLIO

SINCE THE LATE 1960s it has been virtually impossible to divorce the subject of national security policy and basic strategy from that of arms control. In fact, the two have become so intertwined that in some quarters they are regarded as practically synonomous. Even skeptics of arms control have been forced to admit that the issue is a real one, that it attracts significant popular support, and that the agreements reached to date have yielded worthwhile dividends which in certain areas may have helped to restrain the growth of military arsenals. Less clear is what the long-term results of arms control will be—whether limiting weapons will reduce tensions or lessen the risk of war.

Arms control attracts people like Nitze because, as Strobe Talbott observes (borrowing from Clausewitz), it is "defense conducted by other means."[1] Consequently, it is not surprising that one who has been a lifelong advocate of a strong defense has also been among the most active in the arms control field. While doubting that complete and total disarmament is possible, Nitze does not rule out efforts to reach agreements that would approximate this goal. He has no illusions. "We should always be prepared to negotiate," he argues, "but we should also never forget that when we are negotiating with the Soviet Union, we are negotiating with an adversary."[2]

An Unpromising Beginning

In the United States and Europe arms control has been a major concern since the turn of the century. But the contemporary outlines of the problem are distinctly a product of World War II and the advent of nuclear weapons. Soon after it developed and put to use the first atomic bomb, the United States found itself under strong domestic and foreign pressure to make concessions that would, in effect, wipe out its nuclear monopoly. Accordingly, the Truman administration came forth in 1946 with the so-called "Baruch Plan" to halt the production of nuclear weapons and transfer control of all fissionable materials to an international agency that would have authority to conduct on-site inspections of any country's nuclear facilities. This last provision drew a summary rejection from the Soviet Union, which offered a counterproposal that would simply have outlawed nuclear weapons, much as the 1928 Kellogg-Briand Pact had endeavored to outlaw war. Prolonged negotiations ensued but failed to resolve the two most critical issues—inspection and control.

It is tempting to look back upon the late 1940s as years of lost opportunity, as perhaps the last time when negotiated agreements might have eliminated the threat of nuclear war once and for all. But even if by some miracle international control had become a reality, it does not necessarily follow that East-West relations would have improved or that the menace of war would have been completely erased. On the contrary, as Nitze later pointed out, international control was only one problem of many to be resolved. "It needed to be supplemented," he contended,

by concurrent progress in working out other important issues of world politics such as German reunification, a state treaty for Austria, an improved prospect for stability and political progress in the Far East and the Middle East, and a closer balance in nonatomic weapons and military forces between East and West. Atomic security was . . . not separate from, but an integral part of, the general problem of security.[3]

Following Soviet rejection of the Baruch Plan, the Truman administration adopted a wait-and-see attitude toward arms control, while the Soviet Union pressed ahead with its efforts, begun during World War II, to acquire a nuclear capability of its own. Acheson, who had helped draft the report on which the Baruch Plan was based, eventually concluded that arms control was secondary in importance to a general improvement of U.S. strength. Elaborating on Acheson's view, NSC 68 saw limited gains to be made by further arms negotiations and held out little hope of reaching an international control agreement "unless and until the Kremlin design has been frustrated to a point at which a genuine and drastic change in Soviet policies has taken place."[4]

Though NSC 68 devoted several sections to the problems of arms control and disarmament, it did not find the outlook encouraging. Indeed, it felt that the United States would be running a grave risk by not insisting upon substantial concessions from Moscow and a fundamental change in Soviet behavior prior to the signing of any major arms control agreement. Moreover, the report took issue with those who, like George Kennan, felt that a unilateral U.S. declaration of no-first-use of atomic weapons would reduce the danger of a nuclear war. Even though a no-first-use pledge might have propaganda value, NSC 68 dismissed the idea as inconceivable as long as the Soviet Union retained its vast superiority in conventional forces. "Unless we are prepared to abandon our objectives," the report concluded, "we cannot make such a declaration in good faith until we are confident that we will be in a position to attain our objectives without war, or, in the event of war, without recourse to the use of atomic weapons for strategic or tactical purposes."[5] In other words, as long as the United States trailed the Soviets in conventional forces, it could not afford the risk of denying itself the equalizing power of nuclear weapons. Advocates of a no-first-use declaration have continued to plead their case, arguing that such a pledge would provide a definable firebreak against the worldwide disaster of general nuclear war.[6] To be effective, however, a no-first-use policy would mean expenditures for conventional forces well in excess of what any NATO member has ever agreed to consider supporting.

Though the Korean War further dimmed the prospects for arms control, exchanges of views between East and West continued, chiefly through the United Nations, which in November 1951 devoted a special session to the subject of disarmament. In preparation for the session, Nitze and Robert Tufts, a member of the Policy Planning Staff, produced a joint paper in which they raised the possibility of a new U.S. initiative should the opportunity arise. Their operating assumption was that the key to reducing or eliminating nuclear weapons lay in achieving an overall improvement in East-West relations. "International tensions have become so acute and so widespread," they argued, "that it seems unlikely that important progress can be made in any major issue except in the context of a comprehensive approach to the general reduction of tensions." Assuming cooperation from the Soviets and satisfactory progress on a wide range of outstanding issues, Tufts and Nitze suggested that the United States then consider withdrawing the Baruch Plan in favor of some alternative proposal, possibly one with less stringent inspection and control requirements.[7] However, a revised report (NSC 112), prepared as guidance for U.S. negotiators, strongly reaffirmed support for the Baruch Plan or something "no less effective."[8] Doubtless, the point had long since passed when a comprehensive reconciliation of East-West differences could have been negotiated, but it is nevertheless interesting to ponder what the Soviet response to such an offer would have been, especially if it had held out the prospect of greater flexibility on arms control.

A similar offer was in fact finally made by the Eisenhower administration in April 1953, shortly after Stalin's death, when it was thought that new Soviet leadership might be amenable to serious and productive negotiations. Asked to supply ideas, Nitze revived elements of the plan he and Tufts had suggested in 1951 for reducing tensions, merging these with other suggestions provided by Emmet John Hughes into what became Eisenhower's "Chance for Peace" speech: an offer to improve relations, cut back on arms expenditures, and channel the savings into an international fund for aid and reconstruction. The whole project, however, seemed suspect and excessive to Secretary of State Dulles, who made sure that nothing would come of it by stifling the development of concrete follow-on measures. As a result, despite an enthusiastic reception by the press and some signs of interest from Moscow, the speech made little headway and was soon forgotten.[9]

Eisenhower was no doubt sincere in stating repeatedly that he wanted to find ways of curbing the arms race. Unlike Nitze, however, he tended to regard the arms buildup as a major cause of East-West disagreements, and not as a consequence. Eisenhower took the position, therefore, that comprehensive solutions (like the Baruch Plan) that first sought to achieve major improvements in U.S.-Soviet relations were less likely to succeed than piecemeal agreements that attacked the problem directly. Perhaps most successful was his "Atoms for Peace" proposal (December 1953), which offered to share fissionable materials for peaceful research and led in 1957 to the establishment of the International Atomic Energy Agency. Eisenhower also wanted to reduce the risk of surprise attack, and toward this end unveiled his "open skies" plan at the 1955 Geneva summit. Under the proposal, the United States and the Soviet Union would exchange blueprints of their military bases and conduct reconnaissance flights over each other's territory to ensure that aggressive actions were not being planned. Though dismissed at the time by the Soviets as a "crude espionage scheme," they later partially reversed themselves and indicated a willingness to consider aerial reconnaissance arrangements covering a band of Central Europe and a small portion of the Soviet Union.[10] Eventually, with the advent of surveillance satellites, the Soviets retreated even further and conceded that anyone capable of doing so could photograph their country from outer space.

But as committed as Eisenhower may have been, there was an unresolvable conflict between his quest for arms control and his basic approach to national security, with its heavy emphasis on nuclear retaliation. Although the two were not necessarily mutually exclusive, there was obviously a risk that arms control agreements could have adverse effects on national security as long as the United States depended so heavily on nuclear weapons. Basic strategy tended to preclude the negotiation of agreements limiting such weapons. These were further arguments, in Nitze's view, for a change of policy and administration. Arms control, he argued,

depends in part upon what strategy we ourselves consider to be the optimum strategy. If we consider the optimum strategy to be one which puts primary reliance not only upon SAC, but upon its capacity to strike the initial blow . . . then it is very difficult to conceive of any kind of arms control limitation which would not knock that prop out from the support of our national strategy.[11]

With the coming of the Kennedy administration and adoption of the flexible-response doctrine, which downplayed the role of nuclear weapons, Nitze considered the prospects for further arms control agreements substantially improved. The less dependent the United States became on nuclear weapons, he reasoned, the more room it would have to maneuver in negotiations. Even so, Nitze expected no immediate miracles. "As the aggressors," he noted, "the Soviets have less incentive than we since they have little to fear from Western arms as long as they gauge their degree of provocations well."[12] Assuming that the Soviets would continue to behave in this fashion, Nitze viewed arms control arrangements as having two principal functions. First, they should preserve a balance of power that would dissuade the Soviets from reckless action. Second, they should lower the risk of nuclear war or lower the level of damage in such a war should it occur. A third dividend might be a slowing of the arms race, but it did not automatically follow in Nitze's thinking that successful arms control meant a reduction of weapons if such reductions posed a risk to national security or caused the strategic balance to shift in favor of the Soviet Union.

Kennedy and his advisors, including Nitze, saw little chance of a productive dialogue with the Soviets without a firm display of U.S. will and determination, a point of view that further reinforced the need they perceived for a general buildup of U.S. forces. At the same time, however, the administration's attitude may also have served as a barrier to constructive negotiations. Though Kennedy indicated a willingness to explore almost any idea and even established a special organization, the Arms Control and Disarmament Agency (ACDA), to develop and coordinate new proposals, there was virtually no progress in arms control until the Cuban missile crisis underscored the high stakes of a possible U.S.-Soviet confrontation. Thereafter, breakthroughs seemed to occur in rapid succession, but they came in areas of marginal importance where neither side had much to lose or where shared interests happened to converge, as in preventing other countries from acquiring nuclear weapons. By the time the partial nuclear test ban treaty was signed in August 1963, for example, the United States and the Soviet Union had both come close to the practical limits of what could be achieved by atmospheric testing. On many of the questions that remained, experiments underground seemed likely to yield adequate answers.

But if the agreements reached in the 1960s left much to be desired, it was not for lack of trying. In an attempt to move matters along, the Kennedy and Johnson administrations sought to narrow the range of U.S.-Soviet differences by imposing unilateral restraints on the growth of U.S. strategic systems. The earliest restraints were those placed on strategic aircraft—a complete phaseout of the B-47 medium bomber, a gradual reduction of the B-52 fleet, and cancelation of a planned follow-on bomber, the B-70. In addition, Kennedy ordered the withdrawal of all U.S. intermediate-range ballistic missiles (IRBMs) from Turkey, Italy, and the United Kingdom. With the Johnson administration came closer scrutiny of new weapons, such as the controversial antiballistic missile (ABM) defense program, and curbs on systems that might appear to have a first-strike counterforce potential. Indicative of his bias against counterforce, McNamara denied the navy's funding request for an antisubmarine warfare (ASW) capability to hunt down Soviet sea-launched ballistic missiles (SLBMs), and deferred engineering development of such programs as the WS-120-A missile, an early forerunner of the MX, and the Mark 17 nuclear warhead, designed as a highly accurate 1.5 megaton silobuster.[13]

In most cases, to be sure, these decisions had a practical rationale: The weapons involved were either obsolete, unnecessary, or of questionable value as long as the goal of U.S. strategy was assured destruction. Although there was no direct link to arms control per se, the result was basically the same. In effect, it gave the Soviets a chance to catch up, which may have been part of the intention all along. "The Russians," Nitze later remarked, "were not about to enter into negotiations . . . because . . . they thought their position was not close enough to parity and they wouldn't negotiate . . . on any basis other than parity."[14] In other words, until the Soviets improved their bargaining position, it was assumed in Washington that they would have no real incentive to negotiate the fundamental issues. Unilateral restraint helped solve the problem, although in the process the United States may have denied itself improvements in technology that the Soviets were left free to pursue.

The SALT Process

Whatever one might conclude about the arms control policies of the Kennedy and Johnson administrations, it should not be overlooked that they set in motion the process leading to the Strategic Arms Limitation Talks (SALT) of the 1970s. Although SALT was confined to a rather narrow range of problems, many viewed it as a catalyst that, ultimately, would produce a new international order of significantly improved East-West relations. This has not occurred. Indeed, the results have tended to be mixed, sometimes more symbolic than real.

Ironically, SALT originated not in the arms control bureaucracy, but in the Pentagon during the last year or so of McNamara's tenure as secretary of defense. In 1963 Nitze and his naval aide, Capt. Elmo R. Zumwalt, Jr., collaborated on a paper outlining various options for arms reductions under what they termed a "separable first stage disarmament agreement."[15] For McNamara, the impetus to seek such an agreement came from growing evidence that the Soviet Union might be on the verge of deploying a nationwide ABM system, which could pose a serious threat to the U.S. assured destruction capability by the mid-1970s. Although the United States was also developing an anti-ICBM system (thought to be well ahead of the Soviets), it was clear that such a system would entail an enormous investment of resources but provide no definite assurance of increasing American security.

Drawing on the Nitze-Zumwalt paper, McNamara proposed to President Johnson late in 1966 that the United States explore the possibility of talks with the Soviets in order to establish some degree of control over the proliferation of ABMs. The Soviets, exhibiting customary caution, declined to set a date for formal negotiations but indicated that, if and when talks were held, they should address limitations of offensive and defensive nuclear missiles—a somewhat broader spectrum of problems than ABMs. By mid-1968 (at which time the Soviets apparently felt confident that their strategic buildup was meeting its objectives), they offered to open negotiations in conjunction with a planned summit meeting, which President Johnson canceled after the Soviet invasion of Czechoslovakia later that summer. An interest in arms control talks resumed with the arrival of the Nixon administration in 1969. Negotiations would take place in the context of what President Nixon and his national security advisor, Henry Kissinger, conceived as a policy of East-West détente. Finally, in November 1969, negotiations commenced in Helsinki.

To date, the strategic arms talks have yielded three major agreements: the SALT I interim agreement, the ABM treaty (both concluded in 1972), and the ill-fated SALT II accord of 1979, which was never ratified by the United States. Even so, because both sides indicated their willingness to abide by its terms, the effect of the latter agreement was essentially the same as if it had been ratified. In the negotiation of the first two agreements, Nitze played a key role, representing the Office of the Secretary of Defense. As for the SALT II treaty, it is believed in some quarters that Nitze's stinging and persistent criticism of the document was a major factor in the Carter administration's decision to withdraw the treaty from Senate consideration. This probably overstates Nitze's influence, but it is true that he and his associates on the Committee for the Present Danger did wage a vigorous and apparently convincing campaign against the treaty. For this and other reasons, had it come up for a vote in the Senate, the treaty probably would have been defeated.

As involved as Nitze had been in earlier arms control matters, it was not until his appointment to the American SALT delegation in 1969 that he devoted himself full-time to arms control. Going into the talks, Nitze believed they should, at a minimum, enhance "crisis stability" to reduce the temptation on both sides to gain the advantage by launching a first strike during a crisis; and maintain "essential equivalence" between the United States and the Soviet Union in strategic forces.[16] At the initial Helsinki sessions of SALT I, the U.S. delegation dwelled at length on the importance of these goals to both sides so as to prevent the talks from becoming a "zero-sum" game. "We argued," Nitze recalled, "that an agreement which provided essential equivalence, and which maintained or enhanced crisis stability, would add to the security of both sides, reduce the risk of nuclear war, do so at a reduced cost in resources, and thus be of mutual benefit."[17] However, by the summer of 1970 when the talks moved to Vienna, colleagues say Nitze was convinced that the Soviets had worked out a highly one-sided concept of what the talks should accomplish, and that their goal was an agreement that would enhance Soviet power at the expense of the United States.

As the Defense representative on the SALT I delegation, Nitze accorded first importance to the negotiation of effective ABM limitations, even though as deputy secretary of defense and as a private citizen he had been a strong ABM supporter.* The shift in Nitze's thinking came not from any reassessment of the nation's defense needs but from his realization that, politically, the current U.S. ABM was probably doomed in any event. "If the negotiations failed," he found, "we still were not going to have an ABM program because the Senate wasn't going to give it to us."[18] Thus the United States was forced into a weak bargaining position from the start. Moreover, it was unclear what the Soviets proposed to trade in an ABM agreement. Of the two Soviet systems under construction, only the Galosh near Moscow fit the characteristics of an

---

*After leaving government in 1969, Nitze helped organize the Committee to Maintain a Prudent Defense Policy, a lobbying group for ABM. The committee argued that unless Congress backed the ABM program, there would be no reason for the Soviets to agree to limit such systems, a position Nitze carried with him into the SALT negotiations.

ABM. The other, known as Tallinn, was something of a mystery, though U.S. intelligence eventually concluded that it probably was intended as a dual-purpose system, with air defense and ABM capabilities combined.

A more basic difficulty lay in deciding what kinds of ABM restrictions the United States should seek. Initially, the Joint Chiefs of Staff favored limitations on the number of ABM missile interceptors and virtually no limitations on radar tracking systems. This struck Nitze as addressing the wrong problems since interceptors were relatively easy to build and deploy, while radars were not. It seemed advisable therefore to seek an agreement that would cover all possibilities—something that only radar controls could achieve. "If you had already built the radars," Nitze contended, "you could break out rapidly and have a great big system."[19] With safeguards on the testing and deployment of radars, a "breakout" would be practically impossible.

The final ABM treaty, signed in Moscow in 1972, basically encompassed proposals pursued and hammered out in fine detail by Nitze. In addition to restricting both sides to a total of 200 ABM interceptors to be deployed at two separate sites of 100 launchers each,* the agreement imposed close controls on the location and power-aperture product of all phased-array radars, including those not used for ABM. As tightly as the agreement had been drawn, however, Nitze still saw room for improvement and did not seem particularly surprised several years later by reports of suspicious Soviet radar testing. Indeed, the Soviet Union has continued its research and development at an undiminished pace and, in Nitze's view, may today be well along in the deployment of a radar base sufficient for breakout. Nonetheless, the ABM treaty has stood the test of time remarkably well, breathing new life into the mutual-assured-destruction concept while somewhat constraining competition in costly defensive weapons systems.

If the ABM treaty ranks in the judgment of many as a notable success, other products of the SALT process have yet to receive similar accolades, especially from Nitze, who felt that in offensive weapons SALT gave the Soviets definite advantages that continue to prejudice U.S. security. In Nitze's view, a useful agreement on offensive weapons should include controls on the aggregate missile payload, or throwweight, of the forces on both sides, and not just on numbers of missile launchers. In this way, no matter how many launchers or warheads each side might

---

*Reduced to one site each by a protocol signed in 1974 and ratified in 1976.

retain within its ceiling, the other side would always be able to deploy systems denying its adversary a decisive first-strike capability. According to Gerard Smith, who headed the U.S. SALT I delegation, Nitze "constantly pushed in Washington and probed while abroad to see if the scope of the negotiation could not be increased to include controls over throwweight."[20]

One of the most obvious drawbacks to Nitze's approach was, of course, the difficulty of verification. However, with satellite reconnaissance and the other available means of technical surveillance, this problem was hardly insurmountable. Even so, Nitze's proposal received little support from the other delegation members or the agencies they represented back in Washington. The consensus favored simple agreements to begin with, a position that effectively gave preference to negotiating numerical ceilings on launchers as opposed to Nitze's more complicated method of limiting missile characteristics. Such provisions, it was argued, could be fit into future agreements. Nitze had reservations, but because the final treaty on offensive weapons was a five-year interim agreement designed not to foreclose the scope of any replacement agreement, he hoped SALT II could repair any damage that might be done.

SALT I, then, skirted the issue Nitze had raised, leaving the throwweight problem open for future consideration. In fact, it all but eliminated the possibility that the throwweight problem would ever again come up for serious negotiation. Basically, SALT I affirmed the status quo. Its main provision was a "freeze" on the offensive strategic arsenals of both sides at the number of launchers then operational or under construction. In consequence, the Soviets were allowed more launchers as well as superior throwweight, which permitted them to put heavier and more numerous warheads on a single missile. In addition, because the agreement allowed certain modernization measures on both sides, there was little prospect of the Soviets losing their lead. When SALT II commenced, it quickly became apparent that the Soviets, having won what they felt were substantial concessions in the first round, had no interest in relinquishing their advantage. Later on, as Nixon became embroiled in the Watergate affair, he offered further concessions (that is, to substitute an agreement terminating in 1985 for a treaty of indefinite duration) in order to be able to announce a "breakthrough" that would improve his public image. Dismayed with the direction events seemed headed, Nitze resigned from SALT in June 1974.

By the time Nixon finally stepped down from the presidency in August it was generally hoped that SALT would be an ongoing process, moving from one agreement to the next in a steadily progressing reduction of strategic arms. Accordingly, the new Ford administration endeavored to keep the momentum alive by negotiating the Vladivostok agreement of November 1974, which was intended to smooth over the rough spots of SALT I and pave the way for a more permanent SALT II treaty. At their Vladivostok meeting, President Gerald Ford and Soviet leader Leonid Brezhnev agreed to a numerical-parity formula that imposed an overall ceiling on strategic launchers and a sublimit on the number of ICBMs and SLBMs that could be equipped with MIRVs. But as far as Nitze and other like-minded critics were concerned, numerical parity in launchers begged the issue as long as there were no accompanying equalizers, as on throwweight, for example. Furthermore, because the MIRV agreement was nearly impossible to verify with the means permitted, it, too, was less of a breakthrough than it first appeared. On both sides, the presumption remained that any missile capable of being armed with MIRVs would be so armed. Vladivostok also saw the emergence of two other issues—whether to include cruise missiles in future negotiations, and whether to count the new Soviet "Backfire" bomber as a strategic weapon. The haggling over these two questions still continues.

In Nitze's estimation, the SALT II treaty negotiated by the Carter administration compounded the errors and inequities that had worked their way into the earlier SALT I and Vladivostok accords. Many of the charges Nitze leveled against SALT II were highly technical, based on mathematical models that some critics dismissed as too hypothetical to be taken seriously.[21] But for Nitze the evidence was overwhelming that SALT II gave the Soviets a strategic edge they could easily use to change the structure of the global balance of power. "The nuclear balance is only one element in the overall power balance," Nitze recognized. "But in the Soviet view, it is the fulcrum upon which all other levers of influence—military, economic, or political—rest."[22] Where the treaty went astray most seriously, Nitze believed, was in continuing to ignore the throwweight question, thus perpetuating indefinitely Soviet superiority in heavy land-based ICBMs. To Nitze it seemed clear that the Soviets were seeking a true first-strike capability against U.S. land-based systems, a goal that SALT II only helped to further. "SALT II," Nitze concluded, "was not really in our interests. Not that it would hurt us so much [because of prohibitions], but it was an unequal, unfair agreement, full of loopholes, full of inconsistencies, and full of ambiguities."[23]

As chairman of policy studies for the Committee on the Present Danger, Nitze faulted the SALT process for numerous shortcomings, not the least of which, he felt, was its contribution to the steady deterioration of U.S. strength in the 1970s. This charge is difficult to document and, to be sure, much of the evidence is subject to conflicting interpretations.[24] Even so, it is clear that the United States made no real effort to stay abreast of the Soviets, who continued to upgrade and modernize their strategic forces while the United States effectively shelved similar plans of its own. The basic blueprint, known as the Safeguard program (not to be confused with the ABM system of the same name) called for, among other things, the Trident submarine, the B-1 bomber, a new and less vulnerable ICBM (the MX), subsonic cruise missiles, and more powerful warheads for U.S. strategic missiles. But for a variety of reasons—Watergate, the post-Vietnam indifference toward the military, and intensified competition for funds between domestic and national security programs at a time of unprecedented inflation—the Safeguard program was virtually abandoned. A decade went by, during which time defense expenditures slid from 7 percent of GNP in FY 1970 to a post–Korean War low of 4.6 percent in FY 1979. Increases initiated toward the end of the Carter administration and accelerated under President Ronald Reagan have since brought military spending back to a current (FY 1984) level of around 6.6 percent, a figure that accords closely with what Nitze has recommended.[25] But with budget deficits running at record annual levels, no one can safely predict how long the Reagan buildup will last.

All in all, despite high hopes and some early indications of success, the SALT process thus far has failed to produce the more stable and peaceful world order originally envisioned by many of its proponents. With the possible exception of the ABM treaty, the course of the arms race might not have been much different had SALT never occurred. Under the agreements to date, little has been done to reduce the high cost of offensive armaments, and even less seems to have been achieved in creating a structure enhancing stability in a crisis and thus reducing the threat of nuclear war. Furthermore, by continuing the vigorous pursuit of qualitative improvements in their strategic arsenal to buttress their quantitative lead, the Soviets have ably demonstrated that they regard the arms race as far from over, the spirit of SALT notwithstanding. In assessing the direction of the ongoing competition, Nitze believes the net "correlation of forces" is moving in favor of the Soviet Union. "Until this trend changes," he argues, "the prospects for obtaining arms control agreements which would significantly relieve the strain upon the U.S. defense posture are less than good."[26]

The Euromissile Talks

During the 1970s the United States stressed SALT and détente as ways to improve its relations with the Soviet Union. But by the end of the decade, it was far from clear what these policies had accomplished or whether they were still applicable to the evolving international environment. For one thing, the arms control problem had become larger and more diffuse rather than smaller and more manageable. In addition to the continuing competition in strategic systems, a similar race also developed in theater and intermediate-range weapons. At the same time, the long-awaited transformation of Soviet behavior, which détente was supposed to have elicited (Kennan's containment strategy was intended to achieve the same goal) failed to materialize. And though there were signs early in the 1970s of an East-West thaw through such developments as increased East-West trade and the 1972 Berlin agreement, other indications later pointed to a resurgence of Soviet expansionism, with stepped-up penetration in Africa, Southeast Asia, and the Middle East. Depending on how much the United States was prepared to resist, it was entirely possible by the beginning of the 1980s that East and West stood on the threshold of another cold war.

Nowhere were the signs more ominous than in Europe, where hopes for the continuation of a bilateral détente contrasted sharply with the realities of a Soviet military buildup of unprecedented proportions. Part of the buildup was conventional, with more troops, more tanks, and more tactical aircraft added to Warsaw Pact capabilities, which were already numerically superior to opposing NATO forces. But by far the most disturbing development was the improved nuclear capability of the Soviet forces. This trend began in 1974 with the appearance of the Backfire bomber and the introduction two years later of the SS-20 intermediate-range ballistic missile (IRBM) to replace aged Soviet SS-4s and SS-5s. Armed with up to three independently targeted warheads, the

SS-20 had sufficient range to reach any major city in Western Europe from mobile launchpads well inside the Soviet Union. Deployment commenced at the rate of one launcher per week, which gave the Soviets a force of some 180 SS-20 launch systems by the time the Carter administration left office.[27]

Since the Berlin crisis of the early 1960s, NATO commanders had insisted that they needed something comparable to the SS-20 to reach sites in Russia that could rain destruction on Western Europe. As a rule, these requests were ignored in Washington, where decision makers preferred to emphasize the improvement of NATO's conventional capabilities, leaving nuclear missions within Russia to be dealt with by U.S. strategic forces. Nonetheless, the flexible-response doctrine did not mean that NATO or the United States intended to forgo further nuclear options. To the contrary, between 1961 and 1967 the number of U.S. tactical nuclear weapons stockpiled in Europe nearly doubled to more than 7,000, while the United States "assigned" five Polaris submarines to NATO to supplement the small British and French strike forces. On paper, then, the alliance had a rather formidable array of forward-based nuclear systems, though none had the range or yield of Soviet weapons like the SS-20. Consequently, as the Soviet buildup gathered momentum, it put increased pressure on the United States to take some form of countervailing action.

The most concerned were the West Germans, who had no nuclear weapons of their own, but who were likely to be the first victims of any East-West conflict. This latter consideration gave rise to a strident antinuclear movement that expanded rapidly in the late 1970s, to some extent with covert help and encouragement from the Soviet KGB. At the same time West Germans genuinely feared that through the SALT process the United States would bargain away its forward-based systems in Europe and leave Germany defenseless against the threat of a Soviet nuclear attack. Since the 1950s, when Dulles and Adenauer had made policy, U.S.-German collaboration had been the closest in the alliance. By the 1970s that collaboration was showing signs of wear, reflected in frayed relations between Washington and Bonn over the effect of further arms control measures on European security, and the appropriate course NATO should take to counter the military buildup in the East.

In retrospect, it is generally agreed that the opening event in the ensuing controversy was a speech in October 1977 by West German

Chancellor Helmut Schmidt to the International Institute for Strategic Studies in London. Well aware that NATO had already authorized a high-level review of its nuclear requirements, Schmidt pointed to "disparities between East and West in nuclear tactical and conventional weapons," but did not specifically mention the need for a NATO buildup. Rather, he seemed to suggest that a more appropriate solution might be found through the further limitation and reduction of arms, while leaving open the option of improving NATO forces. "But," he added, now moving to his central point:

strategic arms limitations confined to the United States and the Soviet Union will inevitably impair the security of the West European members of the Alliance vis-à-vis Soviet military superiority in Europe if we do not succeed in removing the disparities of military power in Europe parallel to the SALT negotiations. So long as this is not the case we must maintain the balance of the full range of deterrence strategy. The Alliance must, therefore, be ready to make available the means to support its present strategy, which is still the right one, and to prevent any developments that could undermine the basis of this strategy.[28]

Exactly what Schmidt intended by this speech is still rather murky. Obviously, he wanted more progress in arms control, a position in close accord with his earlier endorsements of détente and with his efforts to improve relations between Bonn and Moscow. But he also indicated that, should arms control fail, other ways might have to be found to remove "disparities" caused by the steady increase of Soviet arms. At issue was the reliability of U.S. strategic power in deterring a Soviet attack if in future negotiations the United States made concessions involving its forward-based systems protecting Europe. Although the emphasis throughout the speech was on arms control, Schmidt really seemed to be saying that NATO must have better theater nuclear forces, not only to counter the growing buildup of Soviet SS-20s, but to protect the credibility of deterrence.

NATO wrestled for the next two years with the problems Schmidt had raised. In the end, at its December 1979 meeting, it adopted a decision that surprised no one. Characterizing its proposed actions as "two parallel and complementary approaches," NATO announced plans to modernize and upgrade its intermediate-range nuclear forces (INF) and simultaneously extended an offer to scale back or cancel its modernization program if the Soviets would agree to do likewise with their recently strengthened theater nuclear forces. The modernization measures that NATO endorsed were to begin around the end of 1983 and consist of the deployment of 464 U.S. ground-launched cruise missiles (GLCMs) and 108 U.S. Pershing IIs, each with a range of approximately 1,000 miles, replacing a like number of shorter-range Pershing IAs. The cruise missiles would be dispersed throughout Europe, but all Pershing IIs would be situated in West Germany, an action the Soviets could well have considered provocative.

The NATO decision of December 1979 passed into policy with no great fanfare, but it soon proved to be one of the most controversial in the history of the alliance. Schmidt, whom many regarded as the principal architect of the plan, had been steadily backing away from his 1977 proposals ever since he made them, finding it difficult to convince critics and members of his own political party, the SPD, that the deployment of the new weapons was militarily sound and politically prudent. Indeed, there was every indication that it would add new strains to East-West relations, possibly spelling the demise of détente in Europe while contributing very little to the military security of the alliance. Western military analysts tended to agree that the proposed deployment would be exceedingly expensive and that the benefits derived would not greatly alter the balance of power in Europe. On the whole, however, military concerns had consistently been secondary to political objectives since Schmidt delivered his speech. The deployment decision may not have been necessary from a purely military standpoint, but it was thought necessary to demonstrate the continuing solidarity of the alliance, especially in relations between the Federal Republic of Germany and the United States.

By the time the Reagan administration took office, implementation of the 1979 two-track decision was still pending, though R&D on both the Pershing II and GLCM programs had reached a fairly advanced stage. To save time, it had been decided that R&D and deployment preparations would proceed in tandem. Still unresolved was the question of when talks would begin with the Soviets to fill out the other half of the decision. Liberals in the United States and many in the anti-nuclear movement in Europe doubted Reagan's commitment to arms control, arguing that he was more interested in pursuing a military buildup than in reducing the risk of nuclear war. There was, of course, an element of truth in the charge: Reagan did believe that U.S. defenses had been neglected, and he gave first priority to remedying this situation. But he was also aware of the immense political problems that would arise if the United States backed away from the negotiations or suggested to NATO that it reconsider all or part of its 1979 decision. The die was cast, and in mid-November 1981 Reagan announced his selection of Nitze to head the American negotiating team that would meet with the Soviets in Geneva later that month.

Though he carefully avoided saying so in public, Nitze considered the two-track approach ill-advised, particularly the deployment decision, for it reminded him of the Eisenhower administration's idea of mounting land-based IRBMs aboard mobile launchers to travel the German *Autobahn* disguised as moving vans. The Kennedy administration dropped the scheme and offered instead the creation of a sea-based multinational nuclear force, the MLF, which turned out to have insurmountable problems of its own. To the extent that experience could be any guide in such matters, it was not encouraging.[29]

By far the more immediate problem that Nitze faced was the definition of the negotiating stand the United States should take at Geneva and what he should expect to accomplish. Even the subject of the talks was somewhat cloudy. There was no prior agreement as to what weapons would be covered. The principal American objective, of course, was to rid Europe of the SS-20 threat, though it was also known that there were SS-20s in Asia. Moreover, these were not talks between NATO and the Warsaw Pact, like the Mutual and Balanced Force Reduction (MBFR) negotiations on conventional armaments which had been going on in Vienna since 1973. Rather, they were bilateral negotiations involving only the United States and the Soviet Union. This conformed to Soviet desires, which was somewhat odd in view of Soviet insistence that French and British nuclear systems be taken "into account" as though they were part of the U.S. arsenal. In Washington the presumed purpose of the Soviet proposal was not to reduce or even limit British and French nuclear capabilities, but to eliminate the American INF component and thus attempt to remove Europe from the protection of the U.S. nuclear shield.[30] In any case, Nitze was not authorized to speak for the British and French; throughout the talks he took the position that their forces constituted independent deterrents that did not serve the same function as the American INF.[31]

Going into the Geneva negotiations, Nitze carried with him a proposal that he probably knew had little chance of being accepted—the so-called zero option, an offer to cancel the deployment of American missiles in exchange for the dismantling of all SS-20s. When the offer was made, critics labeled it a blatant and contrived propaganda "gimmick" that showed how little real interest Reagan had in the talks. "It asks the Soviet Union," charged John Newhouse, "to dismantle hundreds of weapons in return for American willingness to forgo a step that may be infeasible in any case."[32] Later, after the talks folded, stories appeared in the press attributing the adoption of the zero-option plan to the influence within U.S. policy circles of an anti–arms control clique, which sought to "put the Soviets on the defensive" and somehow coerce them into accepting an agreement tailored to American interests.[33] While this may be true to some extent, such criticism forgets that the zero option was implicit in the 1979 two-track decision, which envisioned negotiations to eradicate the missile threat on both sides. In this light, the zero option was the inevitable product of the very process that had led to the talks. The proposal might have been inherently flawed, but it had to be tried nonetheless.

Not surprisingly, the Soviets summarily rejected the zero option and tabled proposals of their own predicated on what they termed "equality and equal security." This raised difficulties that were practically insurmountable because the Soviets maintained that a military balance in intermediate-range weapons already existed and that any new U.S. deployments of such weapons, whether cruise missiles or Pershing IIs, would radically alter that balance to the detriment of the Soviet Union. They offered to scale down their SS-20 force in Soviet Europe to a size roughly comparable to the combined British and French nuclear forces. In exchange, the Soviets wanted the United States to drop plans to install Pershing II and cruise missiles in Western Europe. Though the Soviet negotiating position underwent several refinements during the course of the talks, it never veered from opposing the deployment of any new U.S. weapons.

To break the stalemate he saw developing, Nitze in July 1982 initiated a series of informal meetings with his Soviet counterpart, Yuli Kvitsinsky, in an effort to compose "a complete package of reciprocal concessions."[34] Nitze remembered that at SALT I the United States had proposed a similar set of concessions in an attempt to move the talks along but had failed to obtain assurances that the Soviets would reciprocate. In the end, the Soviets simply pocketed the U.S. concessions and insisted the negotiations continue from there. From his SALT experience, Nitze concluded that if the INF talks were to produce an agreement, concessions would have to come from both sides. The result was the celebrated "walk-in-the-woods" formula that would essentially have limited each side to no more than seventy-five missile launchers in Europe, with the Pershing II deployment canceled, and a ceiling of ninety Soviet SS-20 missiles in Asia.

After a scheduled recess, Nitze returned to Geneva in late September eager for Kvitsinsky's report on his government's response to the walk-in-the-woods formula. Reactions in Washington, as Nitze knew, had not been overly enthusiastic, especially in the Pentagon, but there had been no clear-cut rejection of the formula. The main question at home was whether to go along with the proposal to cancel deployment of the Pershing IIs. The Joint Chiefs were divided, but if certain conditions could be met they seemed inclined to waive their objections. Nonetheless, they deemed the issue largely political and declined to offer a formal recommendation. Secretary of Defense Casper Weinberger, on the other hand, strenuously opposed any compromise, as did Assistant Secretary of Defense Richard Perle, who felt that a change at this point would signal a weakening of American resolve. Secretary of State George Shultz seemed to hold no strong views in the matter. The final word belonged, of course, to Reagan. At a meeting of the National Security Council on September 13, 1982, he indicated a preference for holding onto the zero option as long as feasible while deployment of the Pershing IIs proceeded as planned, but he also declined to rule out an agreement that might include features of the walk-in-the-woods approach. Nitze went back to Geneva so instructed.[35]

The breakthrough Nitze had hoped his walk in the woods would produce did not materialize. In Moscow, Kvitsinsky had found less support for the plan than Nitze had found in Washington. Kvitsinsky returned to Geneva severely reprimanded for having overstepped his instructions and shorn of authority to explore a new deal unless Nitze could assure him that his suggestions had been approved by Washington in advance. Having reached an impasse, the talks dragged on inconclusively for nearly a year longer before being broken off at Soviet request in November 1983 just prior to the arrival of the first U.S. cruise missiles in England.

Why the INF talks failed is by no means clear, though several theories have been advanced. One is that bureaucratic politics in Washington sabotaged the negotiations at their most promising point, when the walk-in-the-woods formula might have led to an agreement.* It has since been suggested that if the Reagan administration were only to revive the walk-in-the-woods proposal, the talks could resume immediately and be followed promptly by an agreement.[36] As appealing as this suggestion sounds, however, it overlooks the Soviet attitude toward what constitutes an acceptable settlement. At no time, except for the occasion of Kvitsinsky's lapse during his arboreal walks with Nitze, did the Soviets offer a proposal that did not somehow exclude the deployment of U.S. weapons. From Nitze's standpoint, the walk-in-the-woods formula was as much a trial balloon as anything else. That the Soviets rejected it suggests strongly that they will never be a party to any agreement that sanctions the presence of U.S. forces in Europe.

Although it is highly unlikely that the INF talks will resume, it is still possible that a settlement of sorts may be reached through other channels. This may require, as some have suggested, merging the INF negotiations with the strategic arms reduction talks (START), which have taken the place of SALT, but which, like INF, were suspended in 1983 at Soviet request. The Reagan administration opposes a merger, but it may have no choice if this is the only way the Soviets can be made return to the bargaining table. Alternatively, an entirely new negotiating forum may have to be devised.

Whatever the result, the solution should include provisions for dealing more effectively with Soviet insistence on compensation for British and French nuclear systems. Ultimately, the British and French may have to be included in the talks. During SALT I the Soviets inquired about including British and French systems, but were told that SALT, which was supposed to deal only with strategic weapons, was not an appropriate forum. To the Soviets, anything capable of striking their territory may be classed as a strategic weapon. Thus far, they have used the issue of the British and French missiles largely for propaganda purposes, but they appear to have what many consider a valid point, which makes it doubly effective. As a result, the Western powers have been put in an unfavorable light. In one form or another, the issue must be addressed more positively than it has been in the past.

---

*For a different view that stresses bureaucratic politics in the Kremlin and indecision in Moscow, see John Barry, "Countdown to Breakdown," *Times* (London), November 30, 1983.

By far the greater possibility, however, is that no INF agreement will be reached and that each side will go its own way. At the outset, Nitze sincerely hoped the talks would culminate in a mutually acceptable agreement, although he did realize that the odds against an accord were substantial. The Soviets had already deployed their missiles in large numbers and did not seem inclined to accept an agreement on any terms that the United States and its allies could accept. Now that the talks have been suspended, the Soviets will no doubt continue their propaganda campaign against the Western powers and try to influence European public opinion to block further deployment of U.S. missiles or force NATO to reassess its 1979 decision. It is a situation obviously fraught with danger. Indeed, the prospect of increased turmoil and tension in Europe looms larger today than at any time since the late 1940s.

Nitze's involvement in the INF talks and in the arms control process in general reflects concerns that have been part of his thinking for the past quarter-century or more. In retrospect, Nitze appears convinced that it was a serious mistake for the United States to have lost its strategic superiority late in the 1960s.[37] Were it possible today, he would probably like to see the United States regain that superiority, though being a realist he knows that that is highly unlikely to occur or to be tolerated by the Soviet Union. Consequently, Nitze has devoted his energies and talents to the problems of arms control in an effort to help stem any further erosion in America's strategic posture, focusing on the issues of essential equivalence and crisis stability. At the same time, he has urged continued awareness to the dangers of Soviet expansion, stepped up programs of military preparedness and civil defense, and recognition that arms control agreements by themselves will not buy security. He feels it imperative to maintain channels of contact with the Soviets, but he is averse to negotiating for the sake of negotiating. That the INF talks failed to end in an agreement is for Nitze no doubt a disappointment; but as his reaction to the SALT II treaty indicates, it is better in his opinion to have no agreement at all rather than one that might adversely affect U.S. interests.

The most reliable overall guide to Nitze's thinking is still NSC 68, phrases and concepts from which still appear in his speeches and writings. In Nitze's view and in the concpetion of policy implicit in NSC 68, the U.S.-Soviet relationship is central; all else is secondary. Moreover, it is a relationship between two inherently incompatible sociopolitical systems. The antagonisms and tensions thus generated pose a constant threat to world peace and will continue to do so as long as the Soviet Union evidently remains bent on expanding its power, influence, and ideology. Although NSC 68 did not say that a collision was inevitable, it saw a high possibility that one might occur as long as the United States pursued policies designed to thwart Soviet objectives. In such circumstances, a strengthened defense was a first priority. Thirty-odd years later, Nitze's perspective is basically still the same: "The Kremlin leaders do not want war; they want the world. They believe it unlikely, however, that the West will let them have the world without a fight."[38]

It is possible, of course, as his critics maintain, that Nitze is wrong, that he overestimates the gravity of the Soviet menace, and that he has done so more or less consistently since NSC 68. But as far as Nitze is concerned, our persistent tendency to *underestimate* the Soviet threat has created opportunities that the Soviets have not and will not hesitate to exploit. "If we accept as facts," he argued in 1951, "that the U.S.S.R. is implacably hostile, that they [sic] have dangerously superior relative capabilities for local or limited actions, and that they will act opportunistically, then it seems to me that the unavoidable conclusion is that the U.S.S.R. will exercise their capabilities at any time and place they conceive to be favorable to them."[39] More recently, in surveying the course of Soviet foreign policy since World War II, Nitze found nothing to alter his conviction that Moscow is "doctrinally dedicated to achieving world hegemony," or that the Soviet Union has been willing to invest the necessary resources to realize its goals, even at the expense of its people's well-being and standard of living.[40]

For Nitze, national security is an ongoing problem that ranks above all others, the ultimate test of the American system. Early on, in responding to signs of communist expansion in the late 1940s, the United States committed itself to a policy of containment, which it was hoped, would cause the Russians to change their behavior to something more acceptable. This has not happened, and it was probably wishful thinking to expect that it would. Despite détente and other efforts to improve relations, serious antagonisms have persisted, reinforcing Nitze's contention that East-West differences cannot be easily reconciled. In Nitze's view, containing Soviet expansion should still be the number-one objective of American foreign policy. But it will be no more feasible today than it was in 1950 without increased effort involving sacrifice, dedication, and cooperation from those threatened. In Nitze's thinking, the need for a basic policy modeled on NSC 68 persists and will continue to do so until the nuclear superpowers find a better way to live with one another.

NOTES

Introduction

1. Daniel Yergin, *Shattered Peace: The Origins of the Cold War and the National Security State* (Boston: Houghton, Mifflin, 1978), p. 401.

2. Until a full-scale biography of Nitze appears, source material on Nitze's life and career will remain limited. Among the better profiles of Nitze is the essay by Paul R. Schratz in Paolo E. Coletta, ed., *American Secretaries of the Navy*, 2 vols. (Annapolis, Md.: Naval Institute Press, 1980), II, pp. 941–59, though it deals almost exclusively with Nitze's tenure as secretary of the navy (1963–67). A broader and rather critical biographical sketch of Nitze may also be found in Ronald Brownstein and Nina Easton, *Reagan's Ruling Class* (Washington, D.C.: Presidential Accountability Group, 1982), pp. 518–24. By far the most detailed source on Nitze's early years in business and government is Nitze himself in an interview he gave in 1977 to John N. Dick and James C. Hasdorff as part of the U.S. Air Force oral history program at the Albert F. Simpson Historical Research Center, Maxwell Air Force Base, Alabama.

3. Interview with Nitze by Richard D. McKinzie, July 17, 1975, Arlington, Va., no. 2 in a series, Oral History Collection, Harry S Truman Library, Independence, Mo., p. 8.

4. John Kenneth Galbraith, *A Life in Our Times: Memoirs* (Boston: Houghton, Mifflin, 1981), p. 233 and *passim*.

5. Paul H. Nitze, "Military Power: A Strategic View," *Fletcher Forum* 5 (Winter 1981): 154.

6. United States Strategic Bombing Survey, *Summary Report (Pacific War)* (Washington, D.C.: U.S. Government Printing Office, 1946), pp. 30–32.

Chapter 1. Policy and Strategy for the Cold War

1. The recent release of previously classified State and Defense Department materials has produced a veritable explosion of publications on NSC 68. The most well researched is Samuel F. Wells, Jr., "Sounding the Tocsin: NSC 68 and the Soviet Threat," *International Security* 4 (Fall 1979): 116–58, large parts of which derive from a study Wells wrote for the Defense Department on U.S.-U.S.S.R. strategic arms competition. Also see John Lewis Gaddis, *Strategies of Containment: A Critical Appraisal of Postwar American National Security Policy* (New York: Oxford University Press, 1982), ch. 4; Joseph M. Siracusa, *Rearming for the Cold War: Paul H. Nitze, the H-Bomb, and the Origins of a Soviet First Strike* (Los Angeles: Center for the Study of Armament and Disarmament, 1983); and Sam Postbrief, "Departure from Incrementalism in U.S. Strategic Planning: The Origins of NSC-68," *Naval War College Review* 33 (March–April 1980): 34–57. Earlier accounts, lacking detailed documentation, are less precise but still useful, especially Paul Y. Hammond, "NSC-68: Prologue to Rearmament:" in Warner R. Schilling, Paul Y. Hammond, and Glenn H. Snyder, *Strategy, Politics, and Defense Budgets* (New York: Columbia University Press, 1962), pp. 267–378. Hammond relied principally on interviews and worked closely with Nitze in developing his account.

2. Nitze, "The Relationship of Strategic and Theater Nuclear Forces," *International Security* 2 (Fall 1977): 124–25.

3. "X" [George F. Kennan], "The Sources of Soviet Conduct," *Foreign Affairs* 25 (July 1947): 566–82.

4. For example, Seyom Brown, *The Faces of Power: Constancy and Change in United States Foreign Policy from Truman to Johnson*, pb ed. (New York: Columbia University Press, 1968), ch. 4.

5. Quoted in Walter Millis, ed., *The Forrestal Diaries* (New York: Viking Press, 1951), pp. 350–51.

6. Nitze, "Military Power: A Strategic View," *The Fletcher Forum* 5 (Winter 1981): 160.

7. Nitze, "The Development of NSC 68," *International Security* 4 (Spring 1980): 172.

8. Interview with Nitze by Richard D. McKinzie, August 4, 1975, Northeast Harbor, Maine, no. 3 in a series, Oral History Collection, Harry S Truman Library, Independence, Mo., p. 53.

9. Ibid., p. 129.

10. U.S. Department of State, *Foreign Relations of the United States, 1948*, 9 vols. (Washington, D.C.: U.S. Government Printing Office, 1975), 1:668 (hereafter cited as *FRUS* with appropriate year and volume).

11. Samuel P. Huntington, *The Common Defense: Strategic Programs in National Politics* (New York: Columbia University Press, 1961), p. 41.

12. George F. Kennan, *Memoirs, 1925–50* (Boston: Little, Brown, 1967), pp. 426–27.

13. Charles E. Bohlen, *Witness to History, 1929–1969* (New York: W. W. Norton, 1973), 289–90, and Bohlen's comments on NSC 68 in *FRUS 1950* 1:221–25. Kennan, in his memoirs, makes no mention of NSC 68, as though the paper never existed.

14. Hammond, "Prologue to Rearmament," 287; *FRUS 1950* 1:341–42.

15. Dean Acheson, *Present at the Creation: My Years in the State Department* (New York: W. W. Norton, 1969), p. 374.

16. A summary of WSEG R-1 appears in John Ponturo, *Analytical Support for the Joint Chiefs of Staff: The WSEG Experience, 1948–76* (Arlington, Va.: Institute for Defense Analyses, 1979), pp. 73–74.

17. McKinzie interview with Nitze, p. 8.

18. David S. McLellan, *Dean Acheson: The State Department Years* (New York: Dodd, Mead, 1976), p. 169.

19. *FRUS 1950* 1:141–42.

20. Testimony of Paul H. Nitze, June 17, 1960, in U.S. Congress, Senate Committee on Government Operations, Subcommittee on National Policy Machinery, *Hearings: Organizing for National Security: The Department of State, the Policy Planning Staff, and the National Security Council*, 86th Cong., 2d sess. (Washington, D.C.: U.S. Government Printing Office, 1960), pt. 6, 879.

21. McKinzie interview with Nitze, no. 4, pp. 11, 14.

22. Acheson, *Present at the Creation*, p. 373.

23. "NSC 68: A Report to the National Security Council by the Executive Secretary on United States Objectives and Programs for National Security, April 14, 1950," *Naval War College Review* 27 (May–June 1975): 56.

24. Ibid., p. 64–67.

25. Ibid., p. 99.

26. Ibid., p. 98–101.

27. Ibid., p. 67 and *passim.*

28. United States Strategic Bombing Survey, *Summary Report (Pacific War)* (Washington, D.C.: U.S. Government Printing Office, 1946), pp. 22–25.

29. Interview with Nitze by Walter Miale, April 14, 1976, Personal Papers of Paul H. Nitze (hereafter cited as Nitze Papers).

30. "NSC 68: A Report to the National Security Council," p. 78.

31. Ibid., p. 108.

32. *FRUS 1950,* 1:191.

33. Interview with Nitze by John N. Dick and James C. Hasdorff, part I, October 25–28, 1977, Washington, D.C., U.S. Air Force Oral History Program, p. 247.

34. Acheson, *Present at the Creation,* p. 374. This is not the only inaccuracy in Acheson's account of the processing of NSC 68. Acheson says that the report went to Truman on April 7, 1950, with Johnson's concurrence, and that the president discussed the report with the NSC on April 25. Actually, a preliminary copy of NSC 68 went to Truman on March 31 and it was officially submitted to him on April 11. An NSC meeting was held on April 20 to discuss the report, but Truman did not attend.

35. *FRUS 1950,* 1:400.

36. Ibid., 145–47.

37. Nitze, "The Development of NSC 68," pp. 173–74.

38. Lawton diary entry, May 23, 1950, Papers of Frederick J. Lawton, Harry S Truman Library, Independence, Mo.

39. Office of the Assistant Secretary of Defense (Comptroller), *National Defense Budget Estimates for FY 1984* (U.S. Department of Defense, March 1983), table 7-5.

40. *FRUS 1950,* 1:420.

41. Wells, "Sounding the Tocsin," 141–48.

42. *FRUS 1950,* 7:1326.

Chapter 2: Basic National Security Policy Since NSC 68

1. Memorandum, Eisenhower to Louis Johnson, July 14, 1949, Presidential Papers, Dwight D. Eisenhower Library, Abilene, Kansas.

2. NSC 162/2, October 30, 1953, "Review of Basic National Security Policy," in *United States-Vietnam Relations: 1945–67: Study Prepared by the Department of Defense,* 12 vols. (Washington, D.C.: U.S. Government Printing Office, 1971), 9:178–79. The origins of this policy are addressed by Samuel F. Wells, Jr., in "The Origins of Massive Retaliation," *Political Science Quarterly* 96 (Spring 1981): 31–52; John Lewis Gaddis, *Strategies of Containment* (New York: Oxford University Press, 1982), ch. 5; Glenn H. Snyder, "The New Look of 1953," in Warner R. Schilling, Paul Y. Hammond, and Glenn H. Snyder, *Strategy, Politics, and Defense Budgets* (New York: Columbia University Press, 1962), pp. 379–524; and David Alan Rosenberg, "The Origins of Overkill: Nuclear Weapons and American Strategy, 1945–60," *International Security* 7 (Spring 1983): 3–71.

3. U.S. Department of Defense, *National Defense Budget Estimates for FY 1984* (Washington, D.C.: Office of the Assistant Secretary of Defense [Comptroller], March 1983), tables 6-1 and 7-5.

4. Dwight D. Eisenhower, *The White House Years: Mandate for Change, 1953–1956* (Garden City, N.Y.: Doubleday, 1963), p. 449.

5. Robert J. Art and Kenneth N. Waltz, eds., *The Use of Force: International Politics and Foreign Policy,* 2d ed. (Lanham, Md.: University Press of America, 1983), pp. 142–46.

6. Nitze, "Analysis of Dulles Speech of January 13, 1954 [*sic*], on Security Policy," typescript, Nitze Papers.

7. The official stockpile figures for 1945 to 1948 may be found in David Alan Rosenberg, "U.S. Nuclear Stockpile, 1945 to 1950," *Bulletin of the Atomic Scientists* 38 (May 1982): 25–30. Unofficial numbers are contained in Bernard Brodie, *War and Politics* (New York: Macmillan, 1973), p. 64; and Rosenberg, "Origins of Overkill," p. 23.

8. Wilson quoted in Laurel S. Mayer and Ronald J. Stupak, "The Evolution of Flexible Response in the Post-Vietnam Era," *Air University Review* (November–December 1975): 14.

9. Eisenhower's letter to Richard L. Simon, April 4, 1956, was reprinted in David S. Broder's column "Ike on 'Man Against War,' " *Washington Post,* September 7, 1983.

10. Dwight D. Eisenhower, *The White House Years: Waging Peace, 1956–1961* (Garden City, N.Y.: Doubleday, 1965), p. 467.

11. Barry M. Blechman and Robert Powell, "What in the Name of God is Strategic Superiority?" *Political Science Quarterly* 97 (Winter 1982–83): 589–602; Jerome H. Kahan, *Security in the Nuclear Age: Developing U.S. Strategic Arms Policy* (Washington, D.C.: Brookings Institution, 1975), pp. 18–23; and Gaddis, *Strategies of Containment,* pp. 109–10.

12. Eisenhower, *Mandate for Change,* p. 453.

13. Roger Hilsman, "NATO: The Developing Strategic Context," in Klaus Knorr, ed., *NATO and American Security* (Princeton, N.J.: Princeton University Press, 1959), pp. 9–21.

14. Nitze, "Prospects for a German Settlement," address before Third Annual Institute of the World Affairs Council of Milwaukee, February 21, 1959, Nitze Papers.

15. Nitze, "An Evaluation of Allied Strategy," speech to the Air War College, Maxwell Air Force Base, Alabama, April 20, 1955, Nitze Papers.

16. Nitze, "Atoms, Strategy and Policy," *Foreign Affairs* 34 (January 1956): 187–98.

17. Untitled talking paper prepared by Nitze, dated March 10, 1954, in Defense National Policy (1954) file, Nitze Papers.

18. Fred Kaplan, *The Wizards of Armageddon: Strategists of the Nuclear Age* (New York: Simon and Schuster, 1983), pp. 136–41. Unless otherwise indicated, this section draws on the aforementioned study by Kaplan, chs. 8 and 9, and on Johns Prados, *The Soviet Estimate: U.S. Intelligence Analysis and Russian Military Strength* (New York: Dial Press, 1982), pp. 67–75; Morton H. Halperin, "The Gaither Committee and the Policy Process," *World Politics* 13 (April 1961); and Gaddis, *Strategies of Containment,* pp. 184–87.

19. Kaplan, *Wizards of Armageddon,* pp. 128–29.

20. George B. Kistiakowsky, *A Scientist at the White House* (Cambridge, Mass.: Harvard University Press, 1976), p. 367. Exaggerated Soviet claims appear to have been part of a systematic effort by Moscow to deceive Western intelligence. Michael Mihalka,

"Soviet Strategic Deception, 1955–1981," *Journal of Strategic Studies* 5 (March 1982): 40–93.

21. U.S. Congress, Joint Committee on Defense Production, *Deterrence and Survival in the Nuclear Age (The "Gaither Report" of 1957),* 94th Cong., 2d sess. (Washington, D.C.: U.S. Government Printing Office, 1976), pp. 17–19.

22. Ibid., p. 23.

23. Eisenhower, *Waging Peace,* pp. 221–22.

24. "Power and Policy Problems in the Defense of the West," speech by Paul H. Nitze, April 28, 1960, reprinted in U.S. Congress, Senate Committee on Armed Services, *Hearings: Nominations of Paul H. Nitze and William P. Bundy,* November 7 and 14, 1963, 88th Cong., 1st sess. (Washington, D.C.: U.S. Government Printing Office, 1963), pp. 52–58.

25. Asilomar Press Release, April 28, 1960, Nitze Papers.

26. Quoted in Alain C. Enthoven and K. Wayne Smith, *How Much Is Enough?* (New York: Harper and Row, 1971), p. 122.

27. Theodore C. Sorensen, *Kennedy,* pb. ed., (New York: Harper and Row, 1966), p. 276.

28. Interview with Nitze by Dorothy Fosdick, May 22, 1964, Washington, D.C., John F. Kennedy Oral History Collection, p. 5., John F. Kennedy Library, Boston, Mass.

29. Walt W. Rostow, *The Diffusion of Power: An Essay in Recent History* (New York: Macmillan, 1972), pp. 174–76.

30. Paul H. Nitze, "Presidents and the Development of National Security Policy," in Paul R. Schratz, ed., *Evolution of the American Military Establishment Since World War II* (Lexington, Va.: George C. Marshall Research Foundation, 1978), p. 108.

31. Remarks to the U.S. Civil Defense Council, October 16, 1962, in *Public Statements of Paul H. Nitze, Assistant Secretary of Defense (International Security Affairs), 1961–63,* 2 vols. (Washington, D.C.: Department of Defense, n.d.), 2:306.

32. Remarks to the Democratic Study Luncheon Group, London, England, August 20, 1963; ibid., 2:509.

33. *Hearings: Nitze-Bundy Nominations,* p. 3.

34. Remarks at the Armed Forces Week Luncheon, Philadelphia, May 17, 1953, *Nitze Public Statements,* 2:441.

35. A more detailed examination of the shift in the strategic balance appears in John M. Collins, *American and Soviet Military Trends since the Cuban Missile Crisis* (Washington, D.C.: Center for Strategic and International Studies, Georgetown University, 1978).

36. Art and Waltz, *The Use of Force,* pp. 148–50.

37. Testimony of Robert S. McNamara, January 26, 1967, U.S. Congress, Senate Committee on Armed Service, *Hearings: Military Procurement Authorizations for Fiscal Year 1968,* 90th Cong., 1st sess. (Washington, D.C.: U.S. Government Printing Office, 1967), p. 236. The evolution of the assured destruction concept and the changes that have taken place are described in Desmond Ball, *Targeting for Strategic Deterrence,* Adelphi Papers no. 185 (London: International Institute for Strategic Studies, 1983); and Leon Sloss and Marc Dean Millot, "U.S. Nuclear Strategy in Evolution," *Strategic Review* 12 (Winter 1984): 19–28.

38. Nitze, "The Relationship of Strategic and Theater Nuclear Forces," *International Security* 2 (Fall 1977): 124.

Chapter 3. The Arms Control Imbroglio

1. *Time*, April 18, 1983, p. 17.

2. Nitze, "Strategy in the Decade of the 1980s," *Foreign Affairs* 59 (Fall 1980): 94.

3. Nitze, "U.S. Foreign Policy, 1945–1955," Foreign Policy Association Headline Series, no. 116 (Washington, D.C.: March–April 1956), p. 27.

4. "NSC-68: A Report to the National Security Council . . . on United States Objective and Programs for National Security, April 14, 1950," *Naval War College Review* 27 (May–June 1975): 87.

5. Ibid., p. 84.

6. McGeorge Bundy, George F. Kennan, Robert S. McNamara, and Gerard Smith, "Nuclear Weapons and the Atlantic Alliance," *Foreign Affairs* 60 (Spring 1982): 753–68.

7. U.S., Department of State, *Foreign Relations of the United States, 1951*, 7 vols. (Washington, D.C.: Government Printing Office, 1979), 1:455–63.

8. Ibid., pp. 477–97.

9. Emmet John Hughes, *The Ordeal of Power: A Political Memoir of the Eisenhower Years*, pb. ed. (New York: Atheneum, 1975), pp. 108–15.

10. Glen T. Seaborg, *Kennedy, Khrushchev, and the Test Ban* (Berkeley: University of California Press, 1981), p. 7.

11. Nitze, "Alternate National Strategies and Policies for the U.S.," address to the National War College, December 4, 1959, Nitze Papers.

12. Outline of Nitze; Remarks to the American Bankers Association Monetary Conference, Princeton, N.J., March 6, 1963, *Public Statements of Paul H. Nitze, Assistant Secretary of Defense (International Security Affairs), 1961–63*, 2 vols. (Washington, D.C.: Department of Defense, n.d.), 2:384.

13. Nitze, "SALT II and American Strategic Considerations," *Comparative Strategy* 2 (1980): 22; Jerome H. Kahan, *Security in the Nuclear Age* (Washington, D.C.: Brookings Institution, 1975), pp. 105–109; and interview material.

14. Interview with Nitze by James C. Hasdorff, p. 2, May 19–20, 1981, and July 14–16, 1981, U.S. Air Force Oral History Collection, Maxwell Air Force Base, Alabama, pp. 432–33 (hereafter cited as USAF Interview 2).

15. Elmo R. Zumwalt, Jr., *On Watch: A Memoir* (New York: Quadrangle, 1976), pp. 30–32.

16. Nitze, "The Vladivostok Accord and SALT II," *Review of Politics* 37 (1975): 155.

17. Nitze, "SALT II and American Strategic Considerations," p. 33; also Nitze, "The Strategic Balance Between Hope and Skepticism," *Foreign Policy* 17 (Winter 1974–75): 141–44.

18. USAF Interview 2: 480.

19. Ibid., p. 437.

20. Gerard Smith, *Doubletalk: The Story of the First Strategic Arms Limitations Talks* (Garden City, N.Y.: Doubleday, 1980), p. 41.

21. Alan Tonelson, "Nitze's World," *Foreign Policy* 35 (Summer 1979): 74–90.

22. Nitze, "SALT II and American Strategic Considerations," p. 32.

23. USAF Interview 2: 455.

24. For example, the Committee on the Present Danger's pamphlet, "Does the Official Case for the SALT II Treaty Hold Up Under Analysis?" (March 14, 1979), comparing the committee's views with those of the Carter administration.

25. Nitze, "Military Power: A Strategic View," *Fletcher Forum* 5 (Winter 1981): 156–57.

26. Nitze, "SALT II and American Strategic Considerations," 33–34.

27. Richard J. Barnet, *The Alliance* (New York: Simon and Schuster, 1983), p. 373.

28. Quoted in David N. Schwartz, *NATO's Nuclear Dilemmas* (Washington, D.C.: Brookings Institution, 1983), 214–15.

29. Interview material.

30. Richard Burt, "Prospects for the INF Negotiations," *NATO Review* 30 (February 1983): 1–5.

31. A policy statement appears in Lawrence S. Eagleburger, "Why We Don't Count the French and British Missiles," *Washington Post*, May 8, 1983. Though attributed to Eagleburger, this piece was actually written by Nitze.

32. John Newhouse, "Arms and Allies," *New Yorker*, February 28, 1983, p. 67.

33. Strobe Talbott's account in *Time*, December 5, 1983, p. 19.

34. *New York Times*, January 19, 1984.

35. More detailed accounts appear in Strobe Talbott, "Playing Nuclear Poker," *Time*, January 31, 1983, pp. 10–23; and John P. Wallach, "A Walk in the Woods," *Washingtonian* (January 1984): 61–77.

36. For example, John D. Immele, "A Missile Deal for Europe—and Beyond," *Washington Post*, January 13, 1984.

37. See Nitze's two articles, "Assuring Strategic Stability in an Era of Détente," *Foreign Affairs* 55 (January 1976): 207–32; and "Deterring Our Deterrent," *Foreign Policy* 25 (Winter 1976–77): 195–210.

38. Nitze, "Strategy in the 1980s," p. 90.

39. *FRUS 1951*, 1:174.

40. Nitze, "A Plea for Action," *New York Times Magazine*, May 7, 1978, p. 116 and *passim*.

APPENDIX

NSC 68: A Report to the National Security Council by the Executive Secretary on United States Objectives and Programs for National Security, April 14, 1950

I. BACKGROUNDS OF THE PRESENT WORLD CRISIS

Within the past thirty-five years the world has experienced two global wars of tremendous violence. It has witnessed two revolutions—the Russian and Chinese—of extreme scope and intensity. It has also seen the collapse of five empires—the Ottoman, the Austro-Hungarian, German, Italian and Japanese—and the drastic decline of two major imperial systems, the British and the French. During the span of one generation, the international distribution of power has been fundamentally altered. For several centuries it had proved impossible for any one nation to gain such preponderant strength that a coalition of other nations could not in time face it with greater strength. The international scene was marked by recurring periods of violence and war, but a system of sovereign and independent states was maintained, over which no state was able to achieve hegemony.

Two complex sets of factors have now basically altered this historical distribution of power. First, the defeat of Germany and Japan and the decline of the British and French Empires have interacted with the development of the United States and the Soviet Union in such a way that power has increasingly gravitated to these two centers. Second, the Soviet Union, unlike previous aspirants to hegemony, is animated by a new fanatic faith, antithetical to our own, and seeks to impose its absolute authority over the rest of the world. Conflict has, therefore, become endemic and is waged, on the part of the Soviet Union, by violent or non-violent methods in accordance with the dictates of expediency. With the development of increasingly terrifying weapons of mass destruction, every individual faces the ever-present possibility of annihilation should the conflict enter the phase of total war.

On the one hand, the people of the world yearn for relief from the anxiety arising from the risk of atomic war. On the other hand, any substantial further extension of the area under the domination of the Kremlin would raise the possibility that no coalition adequate to confront the Kremlin with greater strength could be assembled. It is in this context that this Republic and its citizens in the ascendancy of their strength stand in their deepest peril.

89

The issues that face us are momentous, involving the fulfillment or destruction not only of this Republic but of civilization itself. They are issues which will not await our deliberations. With conscience and resolution this Government and the people it represents must now take new and fateful decisions.

II. FUNDAMENTAL PURPOSE OF THE UNITED STATES

The fundamental purpose of the United States is laid down in the Preamble to the Constitution: ". . . to form a more perfect Union, establish Justice, insure domestic Tranquility, provide for the common defence, promote the general Welfare, and secure the Blessings of Liberty to ourselves and our Posterity." In essence, the fundamental purpose is to assure the integrity and vitality of our free society, which is founded upon the dignity and worth of the individual.

Three realities emerge as a consequence of this purpose: Our determination to maintain the essential elements of individual freedom, as set forth in the Constitution and Bill of Rights; our determination to create conditions under which our free and democratic system can live and prosper; and our determination to fight if necessary to defend our way of life, for which as in the Declaration of Independence, "with a firm reliance on the protection of Divine Providence, we mutually pledge to each other our lives, our Fortunes and our sacred Honor."

III. FUNDAMENTAL DESIGN OF THE KREMLIN

The fundamental design of those who control the Soviet Union and the international communist movement is to retain and solidify their absolute power, first in the Soviet Union and second in the areas now under their control. In the minds of the Soviet leaders, however, achievement of this design requires the dynamic extension of their authority and the ultimate elimination of any effective opposition to their authority.

The design, therefore, calls for the complete subversion or forcible destruction of the machinery of government and structure of society in the countries of the non-Soviet world and their replacement by an apparatus and structure subservient to and controlled from the Kremlin. To that end Soviet efforts are now directed toward the domination of the Eurasian land mass. The United States, as the principal center of power in the non-Soviet world and the bulwark of opposition to Soviet expansion, is the principal enemy whose integrity and vitality must be subverted or destroyed by one means or another if the Kremlin is to achieve its fundamental design.

IV. THE UNDERLYING CONFLICT IN THE REALM OF IDEAS AND VALUES BETWEEN THE U.S. PURPOSE AND THE KREMLIN DESIGN

A. Nature of conflict:

The Kremlin regards the United States as the only major threat to the achievement of its fundamental design. There is a basic conflict between the idea of freedom under a government of laws, and the idea of slavery under the grim oligarchy of the Kremlin, which has come to a crisis with the polarization of power described in Section I, and the exclusive possession of atomic weapons by the two protagonists. The idea of freedom, moreover, is peculiarly and intolerably subversive of the idea of slavery. But the converse is not true. The implacable purpose of the slave state to eliminate the challenge of freedom has placed the two great powers at opposite poles. It is this fact which gives the present polarization of power the quality of crisis.

The free society values the individual as an end in himself, requiring of him only that measure of self discipline and self restraint which make the rights of each individual compatible with the rights of every other individual. The freedom of the individual has as its counterpart, therefore, the negative responsibility of the individual not to exercise his freedom in ways inconsistent with the freedom of other individuals and the positive responsibility to make constructive use of his freedom in the building of a just society.

From this idea of freedom with responsibility derives the marvelous diversity, the deep tolerance, the lawfulness of the free society. This is the explanation of the strength of free men. It constitutes the integrity and the vitality of a free and democratic system. The free society attempts to create and maintain an environment in which every individual has the opportunity to realize his creative powers. It also explains why the free society tolerates those within it who would use their freedom to destroy it. By the same token, in relations between nations, the prime reliance of the free society is on the strength and appeal of its idea, and it feels no compulsion sooner or later to bring all societies into conformity with it.

For the free society does not fear, it welcomes, diversity. It derives its strength from its hospitality even to antipathetic ideas. It is a market for free trade in ideas, secure in its faith that free men will take the best wares, and grow to a fuller and better realization of their powers in exercising their choice.

The idea of freedom is the most contagious idea in history, more contagious than the idea of submission to authority. For the breath of freedom cannot be tolerated in a society which has come under the domination of an individual or group of individuals with a will to absolute power. Where the despot holds absolute power—the absolute power of the absolutely powerful will—all other wills must be subjegated in an act of willing submission, a degradation willed by the individual upon himself under the compulsion of a perverted faith. It is the first article of this faith that he finds and can only find the meaning of his existence in serving the ends of the system. The system becomes God, and submission to the will of God becomes submission to the will of the system. It is not enough to yield outwardly to the system—even Ghandian non-violence is not acceptable—for the spirit of resistance and the devotion to a higher authority might then remain, and the individual would not be wholly submissive.

The same compulsion which demands total power over all men within the Soviet state without a single exception, demands total power over all Communist Parties and all states under Soviet domination. Thus Stalin has said that the theory and tactics of Leninism as expounded by the Bolshevik party are mandatory for the proletarian parties of all countries. A true internationalist is defined as one who unhesitatingly upholds the position of the Soviet Union and in the satellite states true patriotism is love of the Soviet Union. By the same token the "peace policy" of the Soviet Union, described at a Party Congress as "a more advantageous form of fighting capitalism" is a device to divide and immobilize the non-Communist world, and the peace the Soviet Union seeks is the peace of total conformity to Soviet policy.

The antipathy of slavery to freedom explains the iron curtain, the isolation, the autarchy of the society whose end is absolute power. The existence and persistence of the idea of freedom is a permanent and continuous threat to the foundation of the slave society; and it therefore regards as intolerable the long continued existence of freedom in the world. What is new, what makes the continuing crisis, is the polarization of power which now inescapably confronts the slave society with the free.

The assault on free institutions is world-wide now, and in the context of the present polarization of power a defeat of free institutions anywhere is a defeat everywhere. The shock we sustained in the destruction of Czechoslovakia was not in the measure of Czechoslovakia's material importance to us. In a material sense, her capabilities were already at Soviet disposal. But when the integrity of Czechoslovak institutions was destroyed, it was in the intangible scale of values that we registered a loss more damaging than the material loss we had already suffered.

Thus unwillingly our free society finds itself mortally challenged by the Soviet system. No other value system is so wholly irreconcilable with ours, so implacable in its purpose to destroy ours, so capable of turning to its own uses the most dangerous and divisive trends in our own society, no other so skillfully and powerfully evokes the elements of irrationality in human nature everywhere, and no other has the support of a great and growing center of military power.

B. Objectives:

The objectives of a free society are determined by its fundamental values and by the necessity for maintaining the material environment in which they flourish. Logically and in fact, therefore, the Kremlin's challenge to the United States is directed not only to our values but to our physical capacity to protect their environment. It is a challenge which encompasses both peace and war and our objectives in peace and war must take account of it.

1. Thus we must make ourselves strong, both in the way in which we affirm our values in the conduct of our national life, and in the development of our military and economic strength.

2. We must lead in building a successfully functioning political and economic system in the free world. It is only by practical affirmation, abroad as well as at home, of our essential values, that we can preserve our own integrity, in which lies the real frustration of the Kremlin design.

3. But beyond thus affirming our values our policy and actions must be such as to foster a fundamental change in the nature of the Soviet system, a change toward which the frustration of the design is the first and perhaps the most important step. Clearly it will not only be less costly but more effective if this change occurs to a maximum extent as a result of internal forces in Soviet society.

In a shrinking world, which now faces the threat of atomic warfare, it is not an adequate objective merely to seek to check the Kremlin design, for the absence of order among nations is becoming less and less tolerable. This fact imposes on us, in our own interests, the responsibility of world leadership. It demands that we make the attempt, and accept the risks inherent in it, to bring about order and justice by means consistent with the principles of freedom and democracy. We should limit our requirement of the Soviet Union to its participation with other nations on the basis of equality and respect for the rights of others. Subject to this requirement, we must with our allies and the former subject peoples seek to create a world society based on the principle of consent. Its framework cannot be inflexible. It will consist of many national communities of great and varying abilities and resources, and hence of war potential. The seeds of conflicts will inevitably exist or will come into being. To acknowledge this is only to acknowledge the impossibility of a final solution. Not to acknowledge it can be fatally dangerous in a world in which there are no final solutions.

All these objectives of a free society are equally valid and necessary in peace and war. But every consideration of devotion to our fundamental values and to our national security demands that we seek to achieve them by the strategy of the cold war. It is only by developing the moral and material strength of the free world that the Soviet regime will become convinced of the falsity of its assumptions and that the pre-conditions for workable agreements can be created. By practically demonstrating the integrity and vitality of our system the free world widens the area of possible agreement and thus can hope gradually to bring about a Soviet acknowledgement of realities which in sum will eventually constitute a frustration of the Soviet design. Short of this, however, it might be possible to create a situation which will induce the Soviet Union to accommodate itself, with or without the conscious abandonment of its design, to coexistence on tolerable terms with the non-Soviet world. Such a development would be a triumph for the idea of freedom and democracy. It must be an immediate objective of United States policy.

There is no reason, in the event of war, for us to alter our over-all objectives. They do not include unconditional surrender, the subjugation of the Russian peoples or a Russia shorn of its economic potential. Such a course would irrevocably unite the Russian people behind the regime which enslaves them. Rather these objectives contemplate Soviet acceptance of the specific and limited conditions requisite to an international environment in which free institutions can flourish, and in which the Russian peoples will have a new chance to work out their own destiny. If we can make the Russian people our allies in this enterprise we will obviously have made our task easier and victory more certain.

The objectives outlined in NSC 20/4 (November 23, 1948) and quoted in Chapter X, are fully consistent with the objectives stated in this paper, and they remain valid. The growing intensity of the conflict which has been imposed upon us, however, requires the changes of emphasis and the additions that are apparent. Coupled with the probable fission bomb capability and possible thermonuclear bomb capability of the Soviet Union, the intensifying struggle requires us to face the fact that we can expect no lasting abatement of the crisis unless and until a change occurs in the nature of the Soviet system.

C. Means:

The free society is limited in its choice of means to achieve its ends. Compulsion is the negation of freedom, except when it is used to enforce the rights common to all. The resort to force, internally or externally, is therefore a last resort for a free society. The act is permissible only when one individual or groups of individuals within it threaten the basic rights of other individuals or when another society seeks to impose its will upon it. The free society cherishes and protects as fundamental the rights of the minority against the will of a majority, because these rights are the inalienable rights of each and every individual.

The resort to force, to compulsion, to the imposition of its will is therefore a difficult and dangerous act for a free society, which is warranted only in the face of even greater dangers. The necessity of the act must be clear and compelling; the act must commend itself to the overwhelming majority as an inescapable exception to the basic idea of freedom; or the regenerative capacity of free men after the act has been performed will be endangered.

The Kremlin is able to select whatever means are expedient in seeking to carry out its fundamental design. Thus it can make the best of several possible worlds, conducting the struggle on those levels where it considers it profitable and enjoying the benefits of a pseudo-peace on those levels where it is not ready for a contest. At the ideological or psychological level, in the struggle for men's minds, the conflict is world-wide. At the political and economic level, within states and in the relations between states, the struggle for power is being intensified. And at the military level, the Kremlin has thus far been careful not to commit a technical breach of the peace, although using its vast forces to intimidate its neighbors, and to support an aggressive foreign policy, and not hesitating through its agents to resort to arms in favorable circumstances. The attempt to carry out its fundamental design is being pressed, therefore, with all means which are believed expedient in the present situation, and the Kremlin has inextricably engaged us in the conflict between its design and our purpose.

We have no such freedom of choice, and least of all in the use of force. Resort to war is not only a last resort for a free society, but it is also an act which cannot definitively end the fundamental conflict in the realm of ideas. The idea of slavery can only be overcome by the timely and persistent demonstration of the superiority of the idea of freedom. Military victory alone would only partially and perhaps only temporarily affect the fundamental conflict, for although the ability of the Kremlin to threaten our security might be for a time destroyed, the resurgence of totalitarian forces and the re-establishment of the Soviet system or its equivalent would not be long delayed unless great progress were made in the fundamental conflict.

Practical and ideological considerations therefore both impel us to the conclusion that we have no choice but to demonstrate the superiority of the idea of freedom by its constructive application, and to attempt to change the world situation by means short of war in such a way as to frustrate the Kremlin design and hasten the decay of the Soviet system.

For us the role of military power is to serve the national purpose by deterring an attack upon us while we seek by other means to create an environment in which our free society can flourish, and by fighting, if necessary, to defend the integrity and vitality of our free society and to defeat any aggressor. The Kremlin uses Soviet military power to back up and serve the Kremlin design. It does not hesitate to use military force agressively if that course is expedient in the achievement of its design. The differences between our fundamental purpose and the Kremlin design, therefore, are reflected in our respective attitudes toward and use of military force.

Our free society, confronted by a threat to its basic values, naturally will take such action, including the use of military force, as may be required to protect those values. The integrity of our system will not be jeopardized by any measures, covert or overt, violent or non-violent, which serve the purposes of frustrating the Kremlin design, nor does the necessity for conducting ourselves so as to affirm our values in actions as well as words forbid such measures, provided only they are appropriately calculated to that end and are not so excessive or misdirected as to make us enemies of the people instead of the evil men who have enslaved them.

But if war comes, what is the role of force? Unless we so use it that the Russian people can perceive that our effort is directed against the regime and its power for aggression, and not against their own interests, we will unite the regime and the people in the kind of last ditch fight in which no underlying problems are solved, new ones are created, and where our basic principles are obscured and compromised. If we do not in the application of force demonstrate the nature of our objectives we will, in fact, have compromised from the outset our fundamental purpose. In the words of the Federalist (No. 28) "The means to be employed must be proportioned to the extent of the mischief." The mischief may be a global war or it may be a Soviet campaign for limited objectives. In either case we should take no avoidable initiative which would cause it to become a war of annihilation, and if we have the forces to defeat a Soviet drive for limited objectives it may well be to our interest not to let it become a global war. Our aim in applying force must be to compel the acceptance of terms consistent with our objectives, and our capabilities for the application of force should, therefore, within the limits of what we can sustain over the long pull, be congruent to the range of tasks which we may encounter.

V. SOVIET INTENTIONS AND CAPABILITIES

A. Political and Psychological.

The Kremlin's design for world domination begins at home. The first concern of a despotic oligarchy is that the local base of its power and authority be secure. The massive fact of the iron curtain isolating the Soviet peoples from the outside world, the repeated political purges within the U.S.S.R. and the institutionalized crimes of the MVD are evidence that the Kremlin does not feel secure at home and that "the entire coercive force of the socialist state" is more than ever one of seeking to impose its absolute authority over "the economy, manner of life, and consciousness of people," (Vyshinski, "The Law of the Soviet State," p. 74). Similar evidence in the satellite states of Eastern Europe leads to the conclusion that this same policy, in less advanced phases, is being applied to the Kremlin's colonial areas.

Being a totalitarian dictatorship, the Kremlin's objective in these policies is the total subjective submission of the peoples now under its control. The concentration camp is the prototype of the society which these policies are designed to achieve, a society in which the personality of the individual is so broken and perverted that he participates affirmatively in his own degradation.

The Kremlin's policy toward areas not under its control is the elimination of resistance to its will and the extension of its influence and control. It is driven to follow this policy because it cannot, for the reasons set forth in Chapter IV, tolerate the existence of free societies; to the Kremlin the most mild and inoffensive free society is an affront, a challenge and a subversive influence. Given the nature of the Kremlin, and the evidence at hand, it seems clear that the ends toward which this policy is directed are the same as those where its control has already been established.

The means employed by the Kremlin in pursuit of this policy are limited only by considerations of expediency. Doctrine is not a limiting factor; rather it dictates the employment of violence, subversion and deceit, and rejects moral considerations. In any event, the Kremlin's conviction of its own infallibility has made its devotion to theory so subjective that past or present pronouncements as to doctrine offer no reliable guide to future actions. The only apparent restraints on resort to war are, therefore, calculations of practicality.

With particular reference to the United States, the Kremlin's strategic and tactical policy is affected by its estimate that we are not only the greatest immediate obstacle which stands between it and world domination, we are also the only power which could release forces in the free and Soviet worlds which could destroy it. The Kremlin's policy toward us is consequently animated by a peculiarly virulent blend of hatred and fear. Its strategy has been one of attempting to undermine the complex of forces, in this country and in the rest of the free world, on which our power is based. In this it has both adhered to doctrine and followed the sound principle of seeking maximum results with minimum risks and commitments. The present application of this strategy is a new form of expression for traditional Russian caution. However, there is no justification in Soviet theory or practice for predicting that, should the Kremlin become convinced that it could cause our downfall by one conclusive blow, it would not seek that solution.

In considering the capabilities of the Soviet world, it is of prime importance to remember that, in contrast to ours, they are being drawn upon close to the maximum possible extent. Also in contrast to us, the Soviet world can do more with less—it has a lower standard of living, its economy requires less to keep it functioning and its military machine operates effectively with less elaborate equipment and organization. The capabilities of the Soviet world are being exploited to the full because the Kremlin is inescapably militant. It is inescapably militant because it possesses and is possessed by a world-wide revolutionary movement, because it is the inheritor of Russian imperialism and because it is a totalitarian dictatorship. Persistent crisis, conflict and expansion are the essence of the Kremlin's militancy. This dynamism serves to intensify all Soviet capabilities.

Two enormous organizations, the Communist Party and the secret police, are an outstanding source of strength to the Kremlin. In the Party, it has an apparatus designed to impose at home an ideological uniformity among its people and to act abroad as an instrument of propaganda, subversion and espionage. In its police apparatus, it has a domestic repressive instrument guaranteeing under present circumstances the continued security of the Kremlin. The demonstrated capabilities of these two basic organizations, operating openly or in disguise, in mass or through single agents, is unparalleled in history. The party, the police and the conspicuous might of the Soviet military machine together tend to create an overall impression of irresistible Soviet power among many peoples of the free world.

The ideological pretensions of the Kremlin are another great source of strength. Its identification of the Soviet system with communism, its peace campaigns and its championing of colonial peoples may be viewed with apathy, if not cynicism, by the oppressed totalitariat of the Soviet world, but in the free world these ideas find favorable responses in vulnerable segments of society. They have found a particularly receptive audience in Asia, especially as the Asiatics have been impressed by what has been plausibly portrayed to them as the rapid advance of the U.S.S.R. from a backward society to a position of great world power. Thus, in its pretensions to being (a) the source of a new universal faith and (b) the model "scientific" society, the Kremlin cynically identifies itself with the genuine aspirations of large numbers of people, and places itself at the head of an international crusade with all of the benefits which derive therefrom.

Finally, there is a category of capabilities, strictly speaking neither institutional nor ideological, which should be taken into consideration. The extraordinary flexibility of Soviet tactics is certainly a strength. It derives from the utterly amoral and opportunistic conduct of Soviet policy. Combining this quality with the elements of secrecy, the Kremlin possesses a formidable capacity to act with the widest tactical latitude, with stealth and with speed.

The greatest vulnerability of the Kremlin lies in the basic nature of its relations with the Soviet people.

That relationship is characterized by universal suspicion, fear and denunciation. It is a relationship in which the Kremlin relies, not only for its power but its very survival, on intricately devised mechanisms of coercion. The Soviet monolith is held together by the iron curtain around it and the iron bars within it, not by any force of natural cohesion. These artificial mechanisms of unity have never been intelligently challenged by a strong outside force. The full measure of their vulnerability is therefore not yet evident.

The Kremlin's relations with its satellites and their peoples is likewise a vulnerability. Nationalism still remains the most potent emotional-political force. The well-known ills of colonialism are compounded, however, by the excessive demands of the Kremlin that its satellites accept not only the imperial authority of Moscow but that they believe in and proclaim the ideological primacy and infallibility of the Kremlin. These excessive requirements can be made good only through extreme coercion. The result is that if a satellite feels able to effect its independence of the Kremlin, as Tito was able to do, it is likely to break away.

In short, Soviet ideas and practices run counter to the best and potentially the strongest instincts of men, and deny their most fundamental aspirations. Against an adversary which effectively affirmed the constructive and hopeful instincts of men and was capable of fulfilling their fundamental aspirations, the Soviet system might prove to be fatally weak.

The problem of succession to Stalin is also a Kremlin vulnerability. In a system where supreme power is acquired and held through violence and intimidation, the transfer of that power may well produce a period of instability.

In a very real sense, the Kremlin is a victim of its own dynamism. This dynamism can become a weakness if it is frustrated, if in its forward thrusts it encounters a superior force which halts the expansion and exerts a superior counterpressure. Yet the Kremlin cannot relax the condition of crisis and mobilization, for to do so would be to lose its dynamism, whereas the seeds of decay within the Soviet system would begin to flourish and fructify.

The Kremlin is, of course, aware of these weaknesses. It must know that in the present world situation they are of secondary significance. So long as the Kremlin retains the initiative, so long as it can keep on the offensive unchallenged by clearly superior counter-force—spiritual as well as material—its vulnerabilities are largely inoperative and even concealed by its successes. The Kremlin has not yet been given real reason to fear and be diverted by the rot within its system.

B. Economic

The Kremlin has no economic intentions unrelated to its overall policies. Economics in the Soviet world is not an end in itself. The Kremlin's policy, in so far as it has to do with economics, is to utilize economic processes to contribute to the overall strength, particularly the war-making capacity of the Soviet system. The material welfare of the totalitariat is severely subordinated to the interests of the system.

As for capabilities, even granting optimistic Soviet reports of production, the total economic strength of the U.S.S.R. compares with that of the U.S. as roughly one to four. This is reflected not only in gross national product (1949: U.S.S.R. $65 billion; U.S. $250 billion), but in production of key commodities in 1949:

	U.S.	U.S.S.R.	U.S.S.R. and European orbit combined
Ingot Steel (million met. tons)	80.4	21.5	28.0
Primary Aluminum (thousand met. tons)	617.6	130–135	140–145
Electric Power (billion kwh.)	410	72	112
Crude Oil (million met. tons)	276.5	33.0	38.9

Assuming the maintenance of present policies, while a large U.S. advantage is likely to remain, the Soviet Union will be steadily reducing the discrepancy between its overall economic strength and that of the U.S. by continuing to devote proportionately more to capital investment than the U.S.

But a full-scale effort by the U.S. would be capable of precipitately altering this trend. The U.S.S.R. today is on a near maximum production basis. No matter what efforts Moscow might make, only a relatively slight change in the rate of increase in overall production could be brought about. In the U.S., on the other hand, a very rapid absolute expansion could be realized. The fact remains, however, that so long as the Soviet Union is virtually mobilized, and the United States has scarcely begun to summon up its forces, the greater capabilities of the U.S. are to that extent inoperative in the struggle for power. Moreover, as the Soviet attainment of an atomic capability has demonstrated, the totalitarian state, at least in time of peace, can focus its efforts on any given project far more readily than the democratic state.

In other fields—general technological competence, skilled labor resources, productivity of labor force, etc.—the gap between the U.S.S.R. and the U.S. roughly corresponds to the gap in production. In the field of scientific research, however, the margin of United States superiority is unclear, especially if the Kremlin can utilize European talents.

C. Military.

The Soviet Union is developing the military capacity to support its design for world domination. The Soviet Union actually possesses armed forces far in excess of those necessary to defend its national territory. These armed forces are probably not yet considered by the Soviet Union to be sufficient to initiate a war which would involve the United States. This excessive strength, coupled now with an atomic capability, provides the Soviet Union with great coercive power for use in time of peace in furtherance of its objectives and serves as a deterrent to the victims of its aggression from taking any action in opposition to its tactics which would risk war.

Should a major war occur in 1950 the Soviet Union and its satellites are considered by the Joint Chiefs of Staff to be in a sufficiently advanced state of preparation immediately to undertake and carry out the following campaigns:

a. To overrun Western Europe, with the possible exception of the Iberian and Scandinavian Peninsulas; to drive toward the oil-bearing areas of the Near and Middle East; and to consolidate Communist gains in the Far East;

b. To launch air attacks against the British Isles and air and sea attacks against the lines of communications of the Western Powers in the Atlantic and the Pacific;

c. To attack selected targets with atomic weapons, now including the likelihood of such attacks against targets in Alaska, Canada, and the United States. Alternatively, this capability, coupled with other actions open to the Soviet Union, might deny the United Kingdom as an effective base of operations for allied forces. It also should be possible for the Soviet Union to prevent any allied "Normandy" type amphibious operations intended to force a reentry into the continent of Europe.

After the Soviet Union completed its initial campaigns and consolidated its positions in the Western European area, it could simultaneously conduct:

a. Full-scale air and limited sea operations against the British Isles;

b. Invasions of the Iberian and Scandinavian Peninsulas;

c. Further operations in the Near and Middle East, continued air operations against the North American continent, and air and sea operations against Atlantic and Pacific lines of communication; and

d. Diversionary attacks in other areas.

During the course of the offensive operations listed in the second and third paragraphs above, the Soviet Union will have an air defense capability with respect to the vital areas of its own and its satellites' territories which can oppose but cannot prevent allied air operations against these areas.

It is not known whether the Soviet Union possesses war reserves and arsenal capabilities sufficient to supply its satellite armies or even its own forces throughout a long war. It might not be in the interest of the Soviet Union to equip fully its satellite armies, since the possibility of defections would exist.

It is not possible at this time to assess accurately the finite disadvantages to the Soviet Union which may accrue through the implementation of the Economic Cooperation Act of 1948, as amended, and the Mutual Defense Assistance Act of 1949. It should be expected that, as this implementation progresses, the internal security situation of the recipient nations should improve concurrently. In addition, a strong United States military position, plus increases in the armaments of the nations of Western Europe, should strengthen the determination of the recipient nations to counter Soviet moves and in event of war could be considered as likely to delay operations and increase the time required for the Soviet Union to overrun Western Europe. In all probability, although United States backing will stiffen their determination, the armaments increase under the present aid programs will not be of any major consequence prior to 1952. Unless the military strength of the Western European nations is increased on a much larger scale than under current programs and at an accelerated rate, it is more than likely that those nations will not be able to oppose even by 1960 the Soviet armed forces in war with any degree of effectiveness. Considering the Soviet Union military capability, the long-range allied military objective in Western Europe must envisage an increased military strength in that area sufficient possibly to deter the Soviet Union from a major war or, in any event, to delay materially the overrunning of Western Europe and, if feasible, to hold a bridgehead on the continent against Soviet Union offensives.

We do not know accurately what the Soviet atomic capability is but the Central Intelligence Agency intelligence estimates, concurred in by State, Army, Navy, Air Force, and Atomic Energy Commission, assign to the Soviet Union a production capability giving it a fission bomb stockpile within the following ranges:

By mid-1950	10–20
By mid-1951	25–45
By mid-1952	45–90
By mid-1953	70–135
By mid-1954	200

This estimate is admittedly based on incomplete coverage of Soviet activities and represents the production capabilities of known or deducible Soviet plants. If others exist, as is possible, this estimate could lead us into a feeling of superiority in our atomic stockpile that might be dangerously misleading, particularly with regard to the timing of a possible Soviet offensive. On the other hand, if the Soviet Union experiences operating difficulties, this estimate would be reduced. There is some evidence that the Soviet Union is acquiring certain materials essential to research on and development of thermonuclear weapons.

The Soviet Union now has aircraft able to deliver the atomic bomb. Our intelligence estimates assign to the Soviet Union an atomic bomber capability already in excess of that needed to deliver available bombs. We have at present no evaluated estimate regarding the Soviet accuracy of delivery on target. It is believed that the Soviets cannot deliver their bombs on target with a degree of accuracy comparable to ours, but a planning estimate might well place it at 40–60 percent of bombs sortied. For planning purposes, therefore, the date the Soviets possess an atomic stockpile of 200 bombs would be a critical date for the United States for the delivery of 100 atomic bombs on targets in the United States would seriously damage this country.

At the time the Soviet Union has a substantial atomic stockpile and if it is assumed that it will strike a strong surprise blow and if it is assumed further that its atomic attacks will be met with no more effective defense opposition than the United States and its allies have programmed, results of those attacks could include:

    a. Laying waste to the British Isles and thus depriving the Western Powers of their use as a base;

    b. Destruction of the vital centers and of the communications of Western Europe, thus precluding effective defense by the Western Powers; and

    c. Delivering devastating attacks on certain vital centers of the United States and Canada.

The possession by the Soviet Union of a thermonuclear capability in addition to this substantial atomic stockpile would result in tremendously increased damage.

During this decade, the defensive capabilities of the Soviet Union will probably be strengthened particularly by the development and use of modern aircraft, aircraft warning and communications devices, and defensive guided missiles.

VI. U.S. INTENTIONS AND CAPABILITIES—ACTUAL AND POTENTIAL

A. Political and Psychological

Our overall policy at the present time may be described as one designed to foster a world environment in which the American system can survive and flourish. It therefore rejects the concept of isolation and affirms the necessity of our positive participation in the world community.

This broad intention embraces two subsidiary policies. One is a policy which we would probably pursue even if there were no Soviet threat. It is a policy of attempting to develop a healthy international community. The other is the policy of "containing" the Soviet system. These two policies are closely interrelated and interact on one another. Nevertheless, the distinction between them is basically valid and contributes to a clearer understanding of what we are trying to do.

The policy of striving to develop a healthy international community is the long-term constructive effort which we are engaged in. It was this policy which gave rise to our vigorous sponsorship of the United Nations. It is of course the principal reason for our long continuing endeavors to create and now develop the Inter-American system. It, as much as containment, underlay our efforts to rehabilitate Western Europe. Most of our international economic activities can likewise be explained in terms of this policy.

In a world of polarized power, the policies designed to develop a healthy international community are more than ever necessary to our own strength.

As for the policy of "containment," it is one which seeks by all means short of war to (1) block further expansion of Soviet power, (2) expose the falsities of Soviet pretensions, (3) induce a retraction of the Kremlin's control and influence and (4) in general, so foster the seeds of destruction within the Soviet system that the Kremlin is brought at least to the point of modifying its behavior to conform to generally accepted international standards.

It was and continues to be cardinal in this policy that we possess superior overall power in ourselves or in dependable combination with other like-minded nations. One of the most important ingredients of power is military strength. In the concept of "containment," the maintenance of a strong military posture is deemed to be essential for two reasons: (1) as an ultimate guarantee of our national security and (2) as an indispensable backdrop to the conduct of the policy of "containment." Without superior aggregate military strength, in being and readily mobilizable, a policy of "containment"—which is in effect a policy of calculated and gradual coercion—is no more than a policy of bluff.

At the same time, it is essential to the successful conduct of a policy of "containment" that we always leave open the possibility of negotiation with the U.S.S.R. A diplomatic freeze—and we are in one now—tends to defeat the very purposes of "containment" because it raises tensions at the same time that it makes Soviet retractions and adjustments in the direction of moderated behavior more difficult. It also tends to inhibit our initiative and deprives us of opportunities for maintaining a moral ascendancy in our struggle with the Soviet system.

In "containment" it is desirable to exert pressure in a fashion which will avoid so far as possible directly challenging Soviet prestige, to keep open the possibility for the U.S.S.R. to retreat before pressure with a minimum loss of face and to secure advantage from the failure of the Kremlin to yield or take advantage of the openings we leave it.

We have failed to implement adequately these two fundamental aspects of "containment." In the face of obviously mounting Soviet military strength ours has declined relatively. Partly as a byproduct of this, but also for other reasons, we now find ourselves at a diplomatic impasse with the Soviet Union, with the Kremlin growing bolder, with both of us holding on grimly to what we have and with ourselves facing difficult decisions.

In examining our capabilities it is relevant to ask at the outset—capabilities for what? The answer cannot be stated solely in the negative terms of resisting the Kremlin design. It includes also our capabilities to attain the fundamental purposes of the United States, and to foster a world environment in which our free society can survive and flourish.

Potentially we have these capabilities. We know we have them in the economic and military fields. Potentially we also have them in the political and psychological fields. The vast majority of Americans are confident that the system of values which animates our society—the principles of freedom, tolerance, the importance of the individual and the supremacy of reason over will—are valid and more vital than the ideology which is the fuel of Soviet dynamism. Translated into terms relevant to the lives of other peoples—our system of values can become perhaps a powerful appeal to millions who now seek or find in authoritarianism a refuge from anxieties, bafflement and insecurity.

Essentially, our democracy also possesses a unique degree of unity. Our society is fundamentally more cohesive than the Soviet system, the solidarity of which is artificially created through force, fear and favor. This means that expressions of national consensus in our society are soundly and solidly based. It means that the possibility of revolution in this country is fundamentally less than that in the Soviet system.

These capabilities within us constitute a great potential force in our international relations. The potential within us of bearing witness to the values by which we live holds promise for a dynamic manifestation to the rest of the world of the vitality of our system. The essential tolerance of our world outlook, our generous and constructive impulses, and the absence of covetousness in our international relations are assets of potentially enormous influence.

These then are our potential capabilities. Between them and our capabilities currently being utilized is a wide gap of unactualized power. In sharp contrast is the situation of the Soviet world. Its capabilities are inferior to those of our Allies and to our own. But they are mobilized close to the maximum possible extent.

The full power which resides within the American people will be evoked only through the traditional democratic process: This process requires, firstly, that sufficient information regarding the basic political, economic and military elements of the present situation be made publicly available so that an intelligent popular opinion may be formed. Having achieved a comprehension of the issues now confronting this Republic, it will then be possible for the American people and the American Government to arrive at a consensus. Out of this common view will develop a determination of the national will and a solid resolute expression of that will. The initiative in this process lies with the Government.

The democratic way is harder than the authoritarian way because, in seeking to protect and fulfill the individual, it demands of him understanding, judgment and positive participation in the increasingly complex and exacting problems of the modern world. It demands that he exercise discrimination: that while pursuing through free inquiry the search for truth he knows when he should commit an act of faith; that he distinguish between the necessity for tolerance and the necessity for just suppression. A free society is vulnerable in that it is easy for people to lapse into excesses—the excesses of a permanently open mind wishfully waiting for evidence that evil design may become noble purpose, the excess of faith becoming prejudice, the excess of tolerance degenerating into indulgence of conspiracy and the excess of resorting to suppression when more moderate measures are not only more appropriate but more effective.

In coping with dictatorial governments acting in secrecy and with speed, we are also vulnerable in that the democratic process necessarily operates in the open and at a deliberate tempo. Weaknesses in our situation are readily apparent and subject to immediate exploitation. This Government therefore cannot afford in the face of the totalitarian challenge to operate on a narrow margin of strength. A democracy can compensate for its natural vulnerability only if it maintains clearly superior overall power in its most inclusive sense.

The very virtues of our system likewise handicap us in certain respects in our relations with our allies. While it is a general source of strength to us that our relations with our allies are conducted on a basis of persuasion and consent rather than compulsion and capitulation, it is also evident that dissent among us can become a vulnerability. Sometimes the dissent has its principal roots abroad in situations about which we can do nothing. Sometimes it arises largely out of certain weaknesses within ourselves, about which we can do something—our native impetuosity and a tendency to expect too much from people widely divergent from us.

The full capabilities of the rest of the free world are a potential increment to our own capabilities. It may even be said that the capabilities of the Soviet world, specifically the capabilities of the masses who have nothing to lose but their Soviet chains, are a potential which can be enlisted on our side.

Like our own capabilities, those of the rest of the free world exceed the capabilities of the Soviet system. Like our own they are far from being effectively mobilized and employed in the struggle against the Kremlin design. This is so because the rest of the free world lacks a sense of unity, confidence and common purpose. This is true in even the most homogeneous and advanced segment of the free world—Western Europe.

As we ourselves demonstrate power, confidence and a sense of moral and political direction, so those same qualities will be evoked in Western Europe. In such a situation, we may also anticipate a general improvement in the political tone in Latin America, Asia and Africa and the real beginnings of awakening among the Soviet totalitariat.

In the absence of affirmative decision on our part, the rest of the free world is almost certain to become demoralized. Our friends will become more than a liability to us; they can eventually become a positive increment to Soviet power.

In sum, the capabilities of our allies are, in an important sense, a function of our own. An affirmative decision to summon up the potential within ourselves would evoke the potential strength within others and add it to our own.

B. Economic

1. **Capabilities.** In contrast to the war economy of the Soviet world (cf. Ch. V-B), the American economy (and the economy of the free world as a whole) is at present directed to the provision of rising standards of living. The military budget of the United States represents 6 to 7 percent of its gross national product (as against 13.8 percent for the Soviet Union). Our North Atlantic Treaty allies devoted 4.8 percent of their national product to military purposes in 1949.

This difference in emphasis between the two economies means that the readiness of the free world to support a war effort is tending to decline relative to that of the Soviet Union. There is little direct investment in production facilities for military end-products and in dispersal. There are relatively few men receiving military training and a relatively low rate of production of weapons. However, given time to convert to a war effort, the capabilities of the United States economy and also of the Western European economy would be tremendous. In the light of Soviet military capabilities, a question which may be a decisive importance in the event of war is the question whether there will be time to mobilize our superior human and material resources for a war effort (cf. Chs. VIII and IX).

The capability of the American economy to support a build-up of economic and military strength at home and to assist a build-up abroad is limited not, as in the case of the Soviet Union, so much by the ability to produce as by the decision on the proper allocation of resources to this and other purposes. Even Western Europe could afford to assign a substantially larger proportion of its resources to defense, if the necessary foundation in public understanding and will could be laid, and if the assistance needed to meet its dollar deficit were provided.

A few statistics will help to clarify this point.

PERCENTAGE OF GROSS AVAILABLE RESOURCES ALLOCATED TO INVESTMENT, NATIONAL DEFENSE, AND CONSUMPTION IN EAST & WEST, 1949
(in percent of total)

Country	Gross investment	Defense	Consumption
U.S.S.R.	25.4	13.8	60.8
Soviet Orbit	22.0[a]	4.0[b]	74.0[a]
U.S.	13.6	6.5	79.9
European NAP [sic] Countries	20.4	4.8	74.8

[a]Crude estimate.

[b]Includes Soviet Zone of Germany; otherwise 5 percent.

The Soviet Union is now allocating nearly 40 percent of its gross available resources to military purposes and investment, much of which is in war-supporting industries. It is estimated that even in an emergency the Soviet Union could not increase this proportion to much more than 50 percent, or by one-fourth. The United States, on the other hand, is allocating only about 20 percent of its resources to defense and investment (or 22 percent including foreign assistance), and little of its investment outlays are directed to war-supporting industries. In an emergency the United States could allocate more than 50 percent of its resources to military purposes and foreign assistance, or five to six times as much as at present.

The same point can be brought out by statistics on the use of important products. The Soviet Union is using 14 percent of its ingot steel, 47 percent of its primary aluminum, and 18.5 percent of its crude oil for military purposes, while the corresponding percentages for the United States are 1.7, 8.6, and 5.6. Despite the tremendously larger production of these goods in the United States than the Soviet Union, the latter is actually using, for military purposes, nearly twice as much steel as the United States and 8 to 26 percent more aluminum.

Perhaps the most impressive indication of the economic superiority of the free world over the Soviet world which can be made on the basis of available data is provided in the following comparisons (based mainly on the Economic Survey of Europe, 1948):

COMPARATIVE STATISTICS ON ECONOMIC CAPABILITIES OF EAST AND WEST

	U.S. 1948–49	European NAT countries 1948–49	Total	U.S.S.R. (1950 Plan)	Satellites 1948–49	Total
Population (millions)	149	173	322	198[a]	75	273
Employment in non-Agricultural Establishments (millions)	45	—	—	31[a]	—	—
Gross National Production (billion dollars)	250	84	334	65[a]	21	86
National Income per capita (current dollars)	1700	480	1040	330	280	315
Production Data[b] Coal (million tons)	582	306	888	250	88	338
Electric Power (billion KWH)	356	124	480	82	15	97
Crude Petroleum (million tons)	277	1	278	35	5	40
Pig Iron (million tons)	5	24	79	19.5	3.2	22.7
Steel (million tons)	80	32	112	25	6	31
Cement (million tons)	35	21	56	10.5	2.1	12.6
Motor Vehicles (thousands)	5273	580	5853	500	25	525

[a]1949 data.

[b]For the European NAT countries and for the satellites, the data include only output by major producers.

It should be noted that these comparisons understate the relative position of the NAT countries for several reasons: (1) Canada is excluded because comparable data were not available; (2) the data for the U.S.S.R. are the 1950 targets (as stated in the fourth five-year plan) rather than actual rates of production and are believed to exceed in many cases the production actually achieved; (3) the data for the European NAT countries are actual data for 1948, and production has generally increased since that time.

Furthermore, the United States could achieve a substantial absolute increase in output and could thereby increase the allocation of resources to a build-up of the economic and military strength of itself and its allies without suffering a decline in its real standard of living. Industrial production declined by 10 percent between the first quarter of 1948 and the last quarter of 1949, and by approximately one-fourth between 1944 and 1949. In March 1950 there were approximately 4,750,000 unemployed, as compared to 1,070,000 in 1943 and 670,000 in 1944. The gross national product declined slowly in 1949 from the peak reached in 1948 ($262 billion in 1948 to an annual rate of $256 billion in the last six months of 1949), and in terms of constant prices declined by about 20 percent between 1944 and 1948.

With a high level of economic activity, the United States could soon attain a gross national product of $300 billion per year, as was pointed out in the President's Economic Report (January 1950). Progress in this direction would permit, and might itself be aided by, a build-up of the economic and military strength of the United States and the free world; furthermore, if a dynamic expansion of the economy were achieved, the necessary build-up could be accomplished without a decrease in the national standard of living because the required resources could be obtained by siphoning off a part of the annual increment in the gross national product. These are facts of fundamental importance in considering the courses of action open to the United States (cf. Ch. IX).

2. Intentions. Foreign economic policy is a major instrument in the conduct of United States foreign relations. It is an instrument which can powerfully influence the world environment in ways favorable to the security and welfare of this country. It is also an instrument which, if unwisely formulated and employed, can do acutal harm to our national interests. It is an instrument uniquely suited to our capabilities, provided we have the tenacity of purpose and the understanding requisite to a realization of its potentials. Finally, it is an instrument peculiarly appropriate to the cold war.

The preceding analysis has indicated that an essential element in a program to frustrate the Kremlin design is the development of a successfully functioning system among the free nations. It is clear that economic conditions are among the fundamental determinants of the will and the strength to resist subversion and aggression.

United States foreign economic policy has been designed to assist in the building of such a system and such conditions in the free world. The principal features of this policy can be summarized as follows:

(1) assistance to Western Europe in recovery and the creation of a viable economy (the European Recovery Program);

(2) assistance to other countries because of their special needs arising out of the war or the cold war and our special interests in or responsibility for meeting them (grant assistance to Japan, the Philippines, and Korea, loans and credits by the Export-Import Bank, the International Monetary Fund, and the International Bank to Indonesia, Yugoslavia, Iran, etc.);

(3) assistance in the development of under-developed areas (the Point IV program and loans and credits to various countries, overlapping to some extent with those mentioned under 2);

(4) military assistance to the North Atlantic Treaty countries, Greece, Turkey, etc.;

(5) restriction of East-West trade in items of military importance to the East;

(6) purchase and stockpiling of strategic materials; and

(7) efforts to re-establish an international economy based on multi-lateral trade, declining trade barriers, and convertible currencies (the GATT-ITO program, the Reciprocal Trade Agreements program, the IMF-IBRD program, and the program now being developed to solve the problem of the United States balance of payments).

In both their short and long term aspects, these policies and programs are directed to the strengthening of the free world and therefore to the frustration of the Kremlin design. Despite certain inadequacies and inconsistencies, which are now being studied in connection with the problem of the United States balance of payments, the United States has generally pursued a foreign economic policy which has powerfully supported its overall objectives. The question must nevertheless be asked whether current and currently projected programs will adequately support this policy in the future, in terms both of need and urgency. and urgency.

The last year has been indecisive in the economic field. The Soviet Union has made considerable progress in integrating the satellite economies of Eastern Europe into the Soviet economy, but still faces very large problems, especially with China. The free nations have important accomplishments to record, but also have tremendous problems still ahead. On balance, neither side can claim any great advantage in this field over its relative position a year ago. The important question therefore becomes: what are the trends?

Several conclusions seem to emerge. First, the Soviet Union is widening the gap between its preparedness for war and the unpreparedness of the free world for war. It is devoting a far greater *proportion* of its resources to military purposes than are the free nations and, in significant components of military power, a greater *absolute* quantity of resources. Second, the Communist success in China, taken with the politico-economic situation in the rest of South and South-East Asia, provides a springboard for a further incursion in this troubled area. Although Communist China faces serious economic problems which may impose some strains on the Soviet economy, it is probable that the social and economic problems faced by the free nations in this area present more than offsetting opportunities for Communist expansion. Third, the Soviet Union holds positions in Europe which, if it maneuvers skillfully, could be used to do great damage to the Western European economy and the the maintenance of the Western orientation of certain countries, particularly Germany and Austria. Fourth, despite (and in part because of) the Titoist defection, the Soviet Union has accelerated its efforts to integrate satellite economy with its own and to increase the degree of autarchy within the areas under its control.

Fifth, meanwhile Western Europe, with American (and Canadian) assistance, has achieved a record level of production. However, it faces the prospect of a rapid tapering off of American assistance without the possibility of achieving, by its own efforts, a satisfactory equilibrium with the dollar area. It has also made very little progress toward "economic integration," which would in the long run tend to improve its productivity and to provide an economic environment conducive to political stability. In particular, the movement towards economic integration does not appear to be rapid enough to provide Western Germany with adequate economic opportunities in the West. The United Kingdom still faces economic problems which may require a moderate but politically difficult decline in the British standard of living or more American assistance than is contemplated. At the same time, a strengthening of the British position is needed if the stability of the Commonwealth is not to be impaired and if it is to be a focus of resistance to Communist expansion in South and South-East Asia. Improvement of the British position is also vital in building up the defensive capabilities of Western Europe.

Sixth, throughout Asia the stability of the present moderate governments, which are more in sympathy with our purposes than any probable successor regimes would be, is doubtful. The problem is only in part an economic one. Assistance in economic development is important as a means of holding out to the peoples of Asia some prospect of improvement in standards of living under their present governments. But probably more important are a strengthening of central institutions, an improvement in administration, and generally a development of an economic and social structure within which the peoples of Asia can make more effective use of their great human and material resources.

Seventh, and perhaps most important, there are indications of a let-down of United States efforts under the pressure of the domestic budgetary situation, disillusion resulting from excessively optimistic expectations about the duration and results of our assistance programs, and doubts about the wisdom of continuing to strengthen the free nations as against preparedness measures in light of the intensity of the cold war.

Eighth, there are grounds for predicting that the United States and other free nations will within a period of a few years at most experience a decline in economic activity of serious proportions unless more positive governmental programs are developed than are now available.

In short, as we look into the future, the programs now planned will not meet the requirements of the free nations. The difficulty does not lie so much in the inadequacy or misdirection of policy as in the inadequacy of planned programs, in terms of timing or impact, to achieve our objectives. The risks inherent in this situation are set forth in the following chapter and a course of action designed to reinvigorate our efforts in order to reverse the present trends and to achieve our fundamental purpose is outlined in Chapter IX.

C. Military.

The United States now possesses the greatest military potential of any single nation in the world. The military weaknesses of the United Sates vis-à-vis the Soviet Union, however, include its numerical inferiority in forces in being and in total manpower. Coupled with the inferiority of forces in being, the United States also lacks tenable positions from which to employ its forces in event of war and munitions power in being and readily available.

It is true that the United States armed forces are now stronger than ever before in other times of apparent peace; it is also true that there exists a sharp disparity between our actual military strength and our commitments. The relationship of our strength to our present commitments, however, is not alone the governing factor. The world situation, as well as commitments, should govern; hence, our military strength more properly should be related to the world situation confronting us. When our military strength is related to the world situation and balanced against the likely exigencies of such a situation, it is clear that our military strength is becoming dangerously inadequate.

If war should begin in 1950, the United States and its allies will have the military capability of conducting defensive operations to provide a reasonable measure of protection to the Western Hemisphere, bases in the Western Pacific, and essential military lines of communication; and an inadequate measure of protection to vital military bases in the United Kingdom and in the Near and Middle East. We will have the capability of conducting powerful offensive air operations against vital elements of the Soviet war-making capacity.

The scale of the operations listed in the preceding paragraph is limited by the effective forces and material in being of the United States and its allies vis-à-vis the Soviet Union. Consistent with the agressive threat facing us and in consonance with overall strategic plans, the United States must provide to its allies on a continuing basis as large amounts of military assistance as possible without serious detriment to United States operational requirements.

If the potential military capabilities of the United States and its allies were rapidly and effectively developed, sufficient forces could be produced probably to deter war, or if the Soviet Union chooses war, to withstand the initial Soviet attacks, to stabilize supporting attacks, and to retaliate in turn with even greater impact on the Soviet capabilities. From the military point of view alone, however, this would require not only the generation of the necessary military forces but also the development and stockpiling of improved weapons of all types.

Under existing peacetime conditions, a period of from two to three years is required to produce a material increase in military power. Such increased power could be provided in a somewhat shorter period in a declared period of emergency or in wartime through a full-out national effort. Any increase in military power in peacetime, however, should be related both to its probable military role in war, to the implementation of immediate and long-term United States foreign policy vis-à-vis the Soviet Union and to the realities of the existing situation. If such a course of increasing our military power is adopted now, the United States would have the capability of eliminating the disparity between its military strength and the exigencies of the situation we face; eventually of gaining the initiative in the "cold" war and of materially delaying if not stopping the Soviet offensives in war itself.

VII. PRESENT RISKS

A. General.

It is apparent from the preceding sections that the integrity and vitality of our system is in greater jeopardy than ever before in our history. Even if there were no Soviet Union we would face the great problem of the free society, accentuated many fold in this industrial age, of reconciling order, security, the need for participation with the requirements of freedom. We would face the fact that in a shrinking world the absence of order among nations is becoming less and less tolerable. The Kremlin design seeks to impose order among nations by means which would destroy our free and democratic system. The Kremlin's possession of atomic weapons puts new power behind its design, and increases the jeopardy to our system. It adds new strains to the uneasy equilibrium-without-order which exists in the world and raises new doubts in men's minds whether the world will long tolerate this tension without moving toward some kind of order, on somebody's terms.

The risks we face are of a new order of magnitude, commensurate with the total struggle in which we are engaged. For a free society there is never total victory, since freedom and democracy are never wholly attained, are always in the process of being attained. But defeat at the hands of the totalitarian is total defeat. These risks crowd in on us, in a shrinking world of polarized power, so as to give us no choice, ultimately, between meeting them effectively or being overcome by them.

B. Specific.

It is quite clear from Soviet theory and practice that the Kremlin seeks to bring the free world under its dominion by the methods of the cold war. The preferred technique is to subvert by infiltration and intimidation. Every institution of our society is an instrument which it is sought to stultify and turn against our purposes. Those that touch most closely our material and moral strength are obviously the prime targets, labor unions, civic enterprises, schools, churches, and all media for influencing opinion. The effort is not so much to make them serve obvious Soviet ends as to prevent them from serving our ends, and thus to make them sources of confusion in our economy, our culture and our body politic. The doubts and diversities that in terms of our values are part of the merit of a free system, the weaknesses and the problems that are peculiar to it, the rights and privileges that free men enjoy, and the disorganization and destruction left in the wake of the last attack on our freedoms, all are but opportunities for the Kremlin to do its evil work. Every advantage is taken of the fact that our means of prevention and retaliation are limited by those principles and scruples which are precisely the ones that give our freedom and democracy its meaning for us. None of our scruples deter those whose only code is, "morality is that which serves the revolution."

Since everything that gives us or others respect for our institutions is a suitable object for attack, it also fits the Kremlin's design that where, with impunity, we can be insulted and made to suffer indignity the opportunity shall not be missed, particularly in any context which can be used to cast dishonor on our country, our system, our motives, or our methods. Thus the means by which we sought to restore our own economic health in the '30's, and now seek to restore that of the free world, come equally under attack. The military aid by which we sought to help the free world was frantically denounced by the Communists in the early days of the last war, and of course our present efforts to develop adequate military strength for ourselves and our allies are equally denounced.

At the same time the Soviet Union is seeking to create overwhelming military force, in order to back up infiltration with intimidation. In the only terms in which it understands strength, it is seeking to demonstrate to the free world that force and the will to use it are on the side of the Kremlin, that those who lack it are decadent and doomed. In local incidents it threatens and encroaches both for the sake of local gains and to increase anxiety and defeatism in all the free world.

The possession of atomic weapons at each of the opposite poles of power, and the inability (for different reasons) of either side to place any trust in the other, puts a premium on a surprise attack against us. It equally puts a premium on a more violent and ruthless prosecution of its design by cold war, especially if the Kremlin is sufficiently objective to realize the improbability of our prosecuting a preventive war. It also puts a premium on piecemeal aggression against others, counting on our unwillingness to engage in atomic war unless we are directly attacked. We run all these risks and the added risk of being confused and immobilized by our inability to weigh and choose, and pursue a firm course based on a rational assessment of each.

The risk that we may thereby be prevented or too long delayed in taking all needful measures to maintain the integrity and vitality of our system is great. The risk that our allies will lose their determination is greater. And the risk that in this manner a descending spiral of too little and too late, of doubt and recrimination, may present us with ever narrower and more desperate alternatives, is the greatest risk of all. For example, it is clear that our present weakness would prevent us from offering effective resistance at any of several vital pressure points. The only deterrent we can present to the Kremlin is the evidence we give that we may make any of the critical points which we cannot hold the occasion for a global war of annihilation.

The risk of having no better choice than to capitulate or precipitate a global war at any of a number of pressure points is bad enough in itself, but it is multiplied by the weakness it imparts to our position in the cold war. Instead of appearing strong and resolute we are continually at the verge of appearing and being alternately irresolute and desperate; yet it is the cold war which we must win, because both the Kremlin design, and our fundamental purpose give it the first priority.

The frustration of the Kremlin design, however, cannot be accomplished by us alone, as will appear from the analysis in Chapter IX, B. Strength at the center, in the United States, is only the first of two essential elements. The second is that our allies and potential allies do not as a result of a sense of frustration or a Soviet intimidation drift into a course of neutrality eventually leading to Soviet domination. If this were to happen in Germany the effect upon Western Europe and eventually upon us might be catastrophic.

But there are risks in making ourselves strong. A large measure of sacrifice and discipline will be demanded of the American people. They will be asked to give up some of the benefits which they have come to associate with their freedoms. Nothing could be more important than that they fully understand the reasons for this. The risks of a superficial understanding or of an inadequate appreciation of the issues are obvious and might lead to the adoption of measures which in themselves would jeopardize the integrity of our system. At any point in this process of demonstrating our will to make good our fundamental purpose, the Kremlin may decide to precipitate a general war, or in testing us, may go too far. These are risks we will invite by making ourselves strong, but they are lesser risks than those we seek to avoid. Our fundamental purpose is more likely to be defeated from lack of the will to maintain it, than from any mistakes we may make or assault we may undergo because of asserting that will. No people in history have preserved their freedom who thought that by not being strong enough to protect themselves they might prove inoffensive to their enemies.

VIII. ATOMIC ARMAMENTS

A. Military Evaluation of U.S. and U.S.S.R. Atomic Capabilities

1. The United States now has an atomic capability, including both numbers and deliverability, estimated to be adequate, if effectively utilized, to deliver a serious blow against the war-making capacity of the U.S.S.R. It is doubted whether such a blow, even if it resulted in the complete destruction of the contemplated target systems, would cause the U.S.S.R. to sue for terms or prevent Soviet forces from occupying Western Europe against such ground resistance as could presently be mobilized. A very serious initial blow could, however, so reduce the capabilities of the U.S.S.R. to supply and equip its military organization and its civilian population as to give the United States the prospect of developing a general military superiority in a war of long duration.

2. As the atomic capability of the U.S.S.R. increases, it will have an increased ability to hit at our atomic bases and installations and thus seriously hamper the ability of the United States to carry out an attack such as that outlined above. It is quite possible that in the near future the U.S.S.R. will have a sufficient number of atomic bombs and a sufficient deliverability to raise a question whether Britain with its present inadequate air defense could be relied upon as an advance base from which a major portion of the U.S. attack could be launched.

It is estimated that, within the next four years, the U.S.S.R. will attain the capability of seriously damaging vital centers of the United States, provided it strikes a surprise blow and provided further that the blow is opposed by no more effective opposition than we now have programmed. Such a blow could so seriously damage the United States as to greatly reduce its superiority in economic potential.

Effective opposition to this Soviet capability will require among other measures greatly increased air warning systems, air defenses, and vigorous development and implementation of a civilian defense program which has been thoroughly integrated with the military defense systems.

In time the atomic capability of the U.S.S.R. can be expected to grow to a point where, given surprise and no more effective opposition than we now have programmed, the possibility of a decisive initial attack cannot be excluded.

3. In the initial phases of an atomic war, the advantages of initiative and surprise would be very great. A police state living behind an iron curtain has an enormous advantage in maintaining the necessary security and centralization of decision required to capitalize on this advantage.

4. For the moment our atomic retaliatory capability is probably adequate to deter the Kremlin from a deliberate direct military attack against ourselves or other free peoples. However, when it calculates that it has a sufficient atomic capability to make a surprise attack on us, nullifying our atomic superiority and creating a military situation decisively in its favor, the Kremlin might be tempted to strike swiftly and with stealth. The existence of two large atomic capabilities in such a relationship might well act, therefore, not as a deterrent, but as an incitement to war.

5. A further increase in the number and power of our atomic weapons is necessary in order to assure the effectiveness of any U.S. retaliatory blow, but would not of itself seem to change the basic logic of the above points. Greatly increased general air, ground and sea strength, and increased air defense and civilian defense programs would also be necessary to provide reasonable assurance that the free world could survive an initial surprise atomic attack of the weight which it is estimated the U.S.S.R. will be capable of delivering by 1954 and still permit the free world to go on to the eventual attainment of its objectives. Furthermore, such a build-up of strength could safeguard and increase our retaliatory power, and thus might put off for some time the date when the Soviet Union could calculate that a surprise blow would be advantageous. This would provide additional time for the effects of our policies to produce a modification of the Soviet system.

6. If the U.S.S.R. develops a thermonuclear weapon ahead of the U.S., the risks of greatly increased Soviet pressure against all the free world, or an attack against the U.S., will be greatly increased.

7. If the U.S. develops a thermonuclear weapon ahead of the U.S.S.R., the U.S. should for the time being be able to bring increased pressure on the U.S.S.R.

B. Stockpiling and Use of Atomic Weapons.

1. From the foregoing analysis it appears that it would be to the long-term advantage of the United States if atomic weapons were to be effectively eliminated from national peacetime armaments; the additional objectives which must be secured if there is to be a reasonable prospect of such effective elimination of atomic weapons are discussed in Chapter IX. In the absence of such elimination and the securing of these objectives, it would appear that we have no alternative but to increase our atomic capability as rapidly as other considerations make appropriate. In either case, it appears to be imperative to increase as rapidly as possible our general air, ground and sea strength and that

of our allies to a point where we are militarily not so heavily dependent on atomic weapons.

2. As is indicated in Chapter IV, it is important that the United States employ military force only if the necessity for its use is clear and compelling and commends itself to the overwhelming majority of our people. The United States cannot therefore engage in war except as a reaction to aggression of so clear and compelling a nature as to bring the overwhelming majority of our people to accept the use of military force. In the event war comes, our use of force must be to compel the acceptance of our objectives and must be congruent to the range of tasks which we may encounter.

In the event of a general war with the U.S.S.R., it must be anticipated that atomic weapons will be used by each side in the manner it deems best suited to accomplish its objectives. In view of our vulnerability to Soviet atomic attack, it has been argued that we might wish to hold our atomic weapons only for retaliation against prior use by the U.S.S.R. To be able to do so and still have hope of achieving our objectives, the non-atomic military capabilities of ourselves and our allies would have to be fully developed and the political weaknesses of the Soviet Union fully exploited. In the event of war, however, we could not be sure that we could move toward the attainment of these objectives without the U.S.S.R.'s resorting sooner or later to the use of its atomic weapons. Only if we had overwhelming atomic superiority and obtained command of the air might the U.S.S.R. be deterred from employing its atomic weapons as we progressed toward the attainment of our objectives.

In the event the U.S.S.R. develops by 1954 the atomic capability which we now anticipate, it is hardly conceivable that, if war comes, the Soviet leaders would refrain from the use of atomic weapons unless they felt fully confident of attaining their objectives by other means.

In the event we use atomic weapons either in retaliation for their prior use by the U.S.S.R. or because there is no alternative method by which we can attain our objectives, it is imperative that the strategic and tactical targets against which they are used be appropriate and the manner in which they are used be consistent with those objectives.

It appears to follow from the above that we should produce stockpile thermonuclear weapons in the event they prove feasible and would add significantly to our net capability. Not enough is yet known of their potentialities to warrant a judgment at this time regarding their use in war to attain our objectives.

3. It has been suggested that we announce that we will not use atomic weapons except in retaliation against the prior use of such weapons by an aggressor. It has been argued that such a declaration would decrease the danger of an atomic attack against the United States and its allies.

In our present situation of relative unpreparedness in conventional weapons, such a declaration would be interpreted by the U.S.S.R. as an admission of great weakness and by our allies as a clear indication that we intended to abandon them. Futhermore, it is doubtful whether such a declaration would be taken sufficiently seriously by the Kremlin to constitute an important factor in determining whether or not to attack the United States. It is to be anticipated that the Kremlin would weigh the facts of our capability far more heavily than a declaration of what we proposed to do with that capability.

Unless we are prepared to abandon our objectives, we cannot make such a declaration in good faith until we are confident that we will be in a position to attain our objectives without war, or, in the event of war, without recourse to the use of atomic weapons for strategic or tactical purposes.

C. International Control of Atomic Energy

1. A discussion of certain of the basic considerations involved in securing effective international control is necessary to make clear why the additional objectives discussed in Chapter IX must be secured.

2. No system of international control could prevent the production and use of atomic weapons in the event of a prolonged war. Even the most effective system of international control could, of itself, only provide (a) assurance that atomic weapons had been eliminated from national peacetime armaments and (b) immediate notice of a violation. In essence, an effective international control system would be expected to assure a certain amount of time after notice of violation before atomic weapons could be used in war.

3. The time period between notice of violation and possible use of atomic weapons in war which a control system could be expected to assure depends upon a number of factors.

The dismantling of existing stockpiles of bombs and the destruction of casings and firing mechanisms could by themselves give little assurance of securing time. Casings and firing mechanisms are presumably easy to produce, even surreptitiously, and the assembly of weapons does not take much time.

If existing stocks of fissionable materials were in some way eliminated and the future production of fissionable materials effectively controlled, war could not start with a surprise atomic attack.

In order to assure an appreciable time lag between notice of violation and the time when atomic weapons might be available in quantity, it would be necessary to destroy all plants capable of making large amounts of fissionable material. Such action would, however, require a moratorium on those possible peacetime uses which call for large quantities of fissionable materials.

Effective control over the production and stockpiling of raw materials might further extend the time period which effective international control would assure. Now that the Russians have learned the technique of producing atomic weapons, the time between violation of an international control agreement and production of atomic weapons will be shorter than was estimated in 1946, except possibly in the field of thermonuclear or other new types of weapons.

4. The certainty of notice of violation also depends upon a number of factors. In the absence of good faith, it is to be doubted whether any system can be designed which will give certainty of notice of violation. International ownership of raw materials and fissionable materials and international ownership and operation of dangerous facilities, coupled with inspection based on continuous unlimited freedom of access to all parts of the Soviet Union (as well as to all parts of the territory of other signatories to the control agreement) appear to be necessary to give the requisite degree of assurance against secret violations. As the Soviet stockpile of fissionable materials grows, the amount which the U.S.S.R. might secretly withhold and not declare to the inspection agency grows. In this sense, the earlier an agreement is consummated the greater the security it would offer. The possibility of successful secret production operations also increases with developments which may reduce the size and power consumption of individual reactors. The development of a thermonuclear bomb would increase many fold the damage a given amount of fissionable material could do and would, therefore, vastly increase the danger that a decisive advantage could be gained through secret operations.

5. The relative sacrifices which would be involved in international control need also to be considered. If it were possible to negotiate an effective system of international control the United States would presumably sacrifice a much larger stockpile of atomic

weapons and a much larger production capacity than would the U.S.S.R. The opening up of national territory to international inspection involved in an adequate control and inspection system would have a far greater impact on the U.S.S.R. than on the United States. If the control system involves the destruction of all large reactors and thus a moratorium on certain possible peacetime uses, the U.S.S.R. can be expected to argue that it, because of greater need for new sources of energy, would be making a greater sacrifice in this regard than the United States.

6. The United States and the peoples of the world as a whole desire a respite from the dangers of atomic warfare. The chief difficulty lies in the danger that the respite would be short and that we might not have adequate notice of its pending termination. For such an arrangement to be in the interest of the United States, it is essential that the agreement be entered into in good faith by both sides and the probability against its violation high.

7. The most substantial contribution to security of an effective international control system would, of course, be the opening up of the Soviet Union, as required under the U.N. plan. Such opening up is not, however, compatible with the maintenance of the Soviet system in its present rigor. This is a major reason for the Soviet refusal to accept the U.N. plan.

The studies which began with the Acheson-Lilienthal committee and culminated in the present U.N. plan made it clear that inspection of atomic facilities would not alone give the assurance of control; but that ownership and operation by an international authority of the world's atomic energy activities from the mine to the last use of fissionable materials was also essential. The delegation of sovereignty which this implies is necessary for effective control and, therefore, is as necessary for the United States and the rest of the free world as it is presently unacceptable to the Soviet Union.

It is also clear that a control authority not susceptible directly or indirectly to Soviet domination is equally essential. As the Soviet Union would regard any country not under its domination as under the potential if not the actual domination of the United States, it is clear that what the United States and the non-Soviet world must insist on, the Soviet Union must at present reject.

The principal immediate benefit of international control would be to make a surprise atomic attack impossible, assuming the elimination of large reactors and the effective disposal of stockpiles of fissionable materials. But it is almost certain that the Soviet Union would not agree to the elimination of large reactors, unless the impracticability of producing atomic power for peaceful purposes had been demonstrated beyond a doubt. By the same token, it would not now agree to elimination of its stockpile of fissionable materials.

Finally, the absence of good faith on the part of the U.S.S.R. must be assumed until there is concrete evidence that there has been a decisive change in Soviet policies. It is to be doubted whether such a change can take place without a change in the nature of the Soviet system itself.

The above considerations make it clear that at least a major change in the relative power positions of the United States and the Soviet Union would have to take place before an effective system of international control could be negotiated. The Soviet Union would have had to have moved a substantial distance down the path of accommodation and compromise before such an arrangement would be conceivable. This conclusion is supported by the Third Report of the United Nations Atomic Energy Commission to the Security Council, May 17, 1948, in which it is stated that " . . . the majority of the Commission has been unable to secure . . . their acceptance of the nature and extent of participation in the world community required of all nations in this field. . . . As a result, the Commission has been forced to recognize that agreement on effective measures for the control of atomic energy is itself dependent on cooperation in broader fields of policy."

In short, it is impossible to hope that an effective plan for international control can be negotiated unless and until the Kremlin design has been frustrated to a point at which a genuine and drastic change in Soviet policies has taken place.

IX. POSSIBLE COURSES OF ACTION

Introduction. Four possible courses of action by the United States in the present situation can be distinguished. They are:

  a. Continuation of current policies, with current and currently projected programs for carrying out these policies;

  b. Isolation;

  c. War; and

  d. A more rapid building up of the political, economic, and military strength of the free world than provided under a, with the purpose of reaching, if possible, a tolerable state of order among nations without war and of preparing to defend ourselves in the event that the free world is attacked.

The role of negotiation. Negotiation must be considered in relation to these courses of action. A negotiator always attempts to achieve an agreement which is somewhat better than the realities of his fundamental position would justify and which is, in any case, not worse than his fundamental position requires. This is as true in relations among sovereign states as in relations between individuals. The Soviet Union possesses several advantages over the free world in negotiations on any issue:

  a. It can and does enforce secrecy on all significant facts about conditions within the Soviet Union, so that it can be expected to know more about the realities of the free world's position than the free world knows about its position;

  b. It does not have to be responsive in any important sense to public opinion;

  c. It does not have to consult and agree with any other countries on the terms it will offer and accept; and

  d. It can influence public opinion in other countries while insulating the people under its control.

These are important advantages. Together with the unfavorable trend of our power position, they militate, as is shown in Section A below, against successful negotiation of a general settlement at this time. For although the United States probably now possesses, principally in atomic weapons, a force adequate to deliver a powerful blow upon the Soviet Union and to open the road to victory in a long war, it is not sufficient by itself to advance the position of the United States in the cold war.

The problem is to create such political and economic conditions in the free world, backed by force sufficient to inhibit Soviet attack, that the Kremlin will accommodate itself to these conditions, gradually withdraw, and eventually change its policies drastically. It has been shown in Chapter VIII that truly effective control of atomic energy would require such an opening up of the Soviet Union and such evidence in other ways of its good faith and its intent to co-exist in peace as to reflect or at least initiate a change in the Soviet system.

Clearly under present circumstances we will not be able to negotiate a settlement which calls for a change in the Soviet system. What, then, is the role of negotiation? In the first place, the public in the United States and in other free countries will require, as a condition to firm policies and adequate programs directed to the frustration of the Kremlin design, that the free world be continuously prepared to negotiate agreements with the Soviet Union on equitable terms. It is still argued by many people here and abroad that equitable agreements with the Soviet Union are possible, and this view will gain force if the Soviet Union begins to show signs of accommodation, even on unimportant issues.

The free countries must always, therefore, be prepared to negotiate and must be ready to take the initiative at times in seeking negotiation. They must develop a negotiating position which defines the issues and the terms on which they would be prepared—and at what stages—to accept agreements with the Soviet Union. The terms must be fair in the view of popular opinion in the free world. This means that they must be consistent with a positive program for peace—in harmony with the United Nations' Charter and providing, at a minimum, for the effective control of all armaments by the United Nations or a successor organization. The terms must not require more of the Soviet Union than such behavior and such participation in a world organization. The fact that such conduct by the Soviet Union is impossible without such a radical change in Soviet policies as to constitute a change in the Soviet system would then emerge as a result of the Kremlin's unwillingness to accept such terms or of its bad faith in observing them.

A sound negotiating position is, therefore, an essential element in the ideological conflict. For some time after a decision to build up strength, any offer of, or attempt at, negotiation of a general settlement along the lines of the Berkeley speech by the Secretary of State could be only a tactic.[1] Nevertheless, concurrently with a decision and a start on building up the strength of the free world, it may be desirable to pursue this tactic both to gain public support for the program and to minimize the immediate risks of war. It is urgently necessary for the United States to determine its negotiating position and to obtain agreement with its major allies on the purposes and terms of negotiation.

In the second place, assuming that the United States in cooperation with other free countries decides and acts to increase the strength of the free world and assuming that the Kremlin chooses the path of accommodation, it will from time to time be necessary and desirable to negotiate on various specific issues with the Kremlin as the area of possible agreement widens.

The Kremlin will have three major objectives in negotiations with the United States. The first is to eliminate the atomic capabilities of the United States; the second is to prevent the effective mobilization of the superior potential of the free world in human

---

[1]The Secretary of State listed seven areas in which the Soviet Union could modify its behavior in such a way as to permit co-existence in reasonable security. These were:
1. Treaties of peace with Austria, Germany, Japan and relaxation of pressures in the Far East;
2. Withdrawal of Soviet forces and influence from satellite area;
3. Cooperation in the United Nations;
4. Control of atomic energy and of conventional armaments;
5. Abandonment of indirect aggression;
6. Proper treatment of official representatives of the U.S.;
7. Increased access to the Soviet Union of persons and ideas from other countries.

and material resources; and the third is to secure a withdrawal of United States forces from, and commitments to, Europe and Japan. Depending on its evaluation of its own strengths and weaknesses as against the West's (particularly the ability and will of the West to sustain its efforts), it will or will not be prepared to make important concessions to achieve these major objectives. It is unlikely that the Kremlin's evaluation is such that it would now be prepared to make significant concessions.

The objectives of the United States and other free countries in negotiations with the Soviet Union (apart from the ideological objectives discussed above) are to record, in a formal fashion which will facilitate the consolidation and further advance of our position, the process of Soviet accommodation to the new political, psychological, and economic conditions in the world which will result from adoption of the fourth course of action and which will be supported by the increasing military strength developed as an integral part of that course of action. In short, our objectives are to record, where desirable, the gradual withdrawal of the Soviet Union and to facilitate that process by making negotiation, if possible, always more expedient than resort to force.

It must be presumed that for some time the Kremlin will accept agreements only if it is convinced that by acting in bad faith whenever and wherever there is an opportunity to do so with impunity, it can derive greater advantage from the agreements than the free world. For this reason, we must take care that any agreements are enforceable or that they are not susceptible of violation without detection and the possibility of effective counter-measures.

This further suggests that we will have to consider carefully the order in which agreements can be concluded. Agreement on the control of atomic energy would result in a relatively greater disarmament of the United States than of the Soviet Union, even assuming considerable progress in building up the strength of the free world in conventional forces and weapons. It might be accepted by the Soviet Union as part of a deliberate design to move against Western Europe and other areas of strategic importance with conventional forces and weapons. In this event, the United States would find itself at war, having previously disarmed itself in its most important weapon, and would be engaged in a race to redevelop atomic weapons.

This seems to indicate that for the time being the United States and other free countries would have to insist on concurrent agreement on the control of non-atomic forces and weapons and perhaps on the other elements of a general settlement, notably peace treaties with Germany, Austria, and Japan and the withdrawal of Soviet influence from the satellites. If, contrary to our expectations, the Soviet Union should accept agreements promising effective control of atomic energy and conventional armaments, without any other changes in Soviet policies, we would have to consider very carefully whether we could accept such agreements. It is unlikely that this problem will arise.

To the extent that the United States and the rest of the free world succeed in so building up their strength in conventional forces and weapons that a Soviet attack with similar forces could be thwarted or held, we will gain increased flexibility and can seek agreements on the various issues in any order, as they become negotiable.

In the third place, negotiation will play a part in the building up of the strength of the free world, apart from the ideological strength discussed above. This is most evident in the problems of Germany, Austria and Japan. In the process of building up strength, it may be desirable for the free nations, without the Soviet Union, to conclude separate arrangements with Japan, Western Germany, and Austria which would enlist the energies and resources of these countries in support of the free world. This will be difficult unless it has been demonstrated by attempted negotiation with the Soviet Union that the Soviet Union is not prepared to accept treaties of peace which would leave these countries free, under adequate safeguards, to participate in the United Nations and in regional or broader associations of states consistent with the United Nations' Charter and providing security and adequate opportunities for the peaceful development of their political and economic life.

This demonstrates the importance, from the point of view of negotiation as well as for its relationship to the building up of the strength of the free world (see Section D below), of the problem of closer association—on a regional or a broader basis—among the free countries.

In conclusion, negotiation is not a possible separate course of action but rather a means of gaining support for a program of building strength, of recording, where necessary and desirable, progress in the cold war, and of facilitating further progress while helping to minimize the risks of war. Ultimately, it is our objective to negotiate a settlement with the Soviet Union (or a successor state or states) on which the world can place reliance as an enforceable instrument of peace. But it is important to emphasize that such a settlement can only record the progress which the free world will have made in creating a political and economic system in the world so successful that the frustration of the Kremlin's design for world domination will be complete. The analysis in the following sections indicates that the building of such a system requires expanded and accelerated programs for the carrying out of current policies.

A. The First Course—Continuation of Current Policies, with Current and Currently Projected Programs for Carrying out These Policies.

1. Military aspects. On the basis of current programs, the United States has a large potential military capability but an actual capability which, though improving, is declining relative to the U.S.S.R., particularly in light of its probable fission bomb capability and possible thermonuclear bomb capability. The same holds true for the free world as a whole relative to the Soviet world as a whole. If war breaks out in 1950 or in the next few years, the United States and its allies, apart from a powerful atomic blow, will be compelled to conduct delaying actions, while building up their strength for a general offensive. A frank evaluation of the requirements, to defend the United States and its vital interests and to support a vigorous initiative in the cold war, on the one hand, and of present capabilities, on the other, indicates that there is a sharp and growing disparity between them.

A review of Soviet policy shows that the military capabilities, actual and potential, of the United States and the rest of the free world, together with the apparent determination of the free world to resist further Soviet expansion, have not induced the Kremlin to relax its pressures generally or to give up the initiative in the cold war. On the contrary, the Soviet Union has consistently pursued a bold foreign policy, modified only when its probing revealed a determination and an ability of the free world to resist encroachment upon it. The relative military capabilities of the free world are declining, with the result that its determination to resist may also decline and that the security of the United States and the free world as a whole will be jeopardized.

From the military point of view, the actual and potential capabilities of the United States, given a continuation of current and projected programs, will become less and less effective as a war deterrent. Improvement of the state of readiness will become more and more important not only to inhibit the launching of war by the Soviet Union but also to support a national policy designed to reverse the present ominous trends in international relations. A building up of the military capabilities of the United States and the free world is a precondition to the achievement of the objectives outlined in this report and to the protection of the United States against disaster.

Fortunately, the United States military establishment has been developed into a unified and effective force as a result of the policies laid down by the Congress and the vigorous carrying out of these policies by the Administration in the fields of both organization and economy. It is, therefore, a base upon which increased strength can be rapidly built with maximum efficiency and economy.

2. Political aspects. The Soviet Union is pursuing the initiative in the conflict with the free world. Its atomic capabilities, together with its successes in the Far East, have led to an increasing confidence on its part and to an increasing nervousness in Western Europe and the rest of the free world. We cannot be sure, of course, how vigorously the Soviet Union will pursue its initiative, nor can we be sure of the strength or weakness of the other free countries in reacting to it. There are, however, ominous signs of further deterioration in the Far East. There are also some indications that a decline in morale and confidence in Western Europe may be expected. In particular, the situation in Germany is unsettled. Should the belief or suspicion spread that the free nations are not now able to prevent the Soviet Union from taking, if it chooses, the military actions outlined in Chapter V, the determination of the free countries to resist probably would lessen and there would be an increasing temptation for them to seek a position of neutrality.

Politically, recognition of the military implications of a continuation of present trends will mean that the United States and especially other free countries will tend to shift to the defensive, or to follow a dangerous policy of bluff, because the maintenance of a firm initiative in the cold war is closely related to aggregate strength in being and readily available.

This is largely a problem of the incongruity of the current actual capabilities of the free world and the threat to it, for the free world has an economic and military potential far superior to the potential of the Soviet Union and its satellites. The shadow of Soviet force falls darkly on Western Europe and Asia and supports a policy of encroachment. The free world lacks adequate means—in the form of forces in being—to thwart such expansion locally. The United States will therefore be confronted more frequently with the dilemma of reacting totally to a limited extension of Soviet control or of not reacting at all (except with ineffectual protests and half measures). Continuation of present trends is likely to lead, therefore, to a gradual withdrawal under the direct or indirect pressure of the Soviet Union, until we discover one day that we have sacrificed positions of vital interest. In other words, the United States would have chosen, by lack of the necessary decisions and actions, to fall back to isolation in the Western Hemisphere. This course would at best result in only a relatively brief truce and would be ended either by our capitulation or by a defensive war—on unfavorable terms from unfavorable positions—against a Soviet Empire comprising all or most of Eurasia. (See Section B.)

3. Economic and social aspects. As was pointed out in Chapter VI, the present foreign economic policies and programs of the United States will not produce a solution to the problem of international economic equilibrium, notably the problem of the dollar gap, and will not create an economic base conducive to political stability in many important free countries.

The European Recovery Program has been successful in assisting the restoration and expansion of production in Western Europe and has been a major factor in checking the dry rot of Communism in Western Europe. However, little progress has been made toward the resumption by Western Europe of a position of influence in world affairs commensurate with its potential strength. Progress in this direction will require integrated political, economic and military policies and programs, which are supported by the United States and the Western European countries and which will probably require a deeper participation by the United States than has been contemplated.

The Point IV Program and other assistance programs will not adequately supplement, as now projected, the efforts of other important countries to develop effective institutions, to improve the administration of their affairs, and to achieve a sufficient measure of economic development. The moderate regimes now in power in many countries, like India, Indonesia, Pakistan, and the Philippines, will probably be unable to restore or retain their popular support and authority unless they are assisted in bringing about a more rapid improvement of the economic and social structure than present programs will make possible.

The Executive Branch is now undertaking a study of the problem of the United States balance of payments and of the measures which might be taken by the United States to assist in establishing international economic equilibrium. This is a very important project and work on it should have a high priority. However, unless such an economic program is matched and supplemented by an equally far-sighted and vigorous political and military program, we will not be successful in checking and rolling back the Kremlin's drive.

4. Negotiation. In short, by continuing along its present course the free world will not succeed in making effective use of its vastly superior political, economic, and military potential to build a tolerable state of order among nations. On the contrary, the political, economic and military situation of the free world is already unsatisfactory and will become less favorable unless we act to reverse present trends.

This situation is one which militates against successful negotiations with the Kremlin—for the terms of agreements on important pending issues would reflect present realities and would therefore be unacceptable, if not disastrous, to the United States and the rest of the free world. Unless a decision had been made and action undertaken to build up the strength, in the broadest sense, of the United States and the free world, an attempt to negotiate a general settlement on terms acceptable to us would be ineffective and probably long drawn out, and might thereby seriously delay the necessary measures to build up our strength.

This is true despite the fact that the United States now has the capability of delivering a powerful blow against the Soviet Union in the event of war, for one of the present realities is that the United States is not prepared to threaten the use of our present atomic superiority to coerce the Soviet Union into acceptable agreements. In light of present trends, the Soviet Union will not withdraw and the only conceivable basis for a general settlement would be spheres of influence and of no influence—a "settlement" which the Kremlin could readily exploit to its great advantage. The idea that Germany or Japan or other important areas can exist as islands of neutrality in a divided world is unreal, given the Kremlin design for world domination.

B. The Second Course—Isolation.

Continuation of present trends, it has been shown above, will lead progressively to the withdrawal of the United States from most of its present commitments in Europe and Asia and to our isolation in the Western Hemisphere and its approaches. This would result not from a conscious decision but from a failure to take the actions necessary to bring our capabilities into line with our commitments and thus to a withdrawal under pressure. This pressure might come from our present Allies, who will tend to seek other "solutions" unless they have confidence in our determination to accelerate our efforts to build a successfully functioning political and economic system in the free world.

There are some who advocate a deliberate decision to isolate ourselves. Superficially, this has some attractiveness as a course of action, for it appears to bring our commitments and capabilities into harmony by reducing the former and by concentrating our present, or perhaps even reduced, military expenditures on the defense of the United States.

This argument overlooks the relativity of capabilities. With the United States in an isolated position, we would have to face the probability that the Soviet Union would quickly dominate most of Eurasia, probably without meeting armed resistance. It would thus acquire a potential far superior to our own, and would promptly proceed to develop this potential with the purpose of eliminating our power, which would, even in isolation, remain as a challenge to it and as an obstacle to the imposition of its kind of order in the world. There is no way to make ourselves inoffensive to the Kremlin except by complete submission to its will. Therefore isolation would in the end condemn us to capitulate or to fight alone and on the defensive, with drastically limited offensive and retaliatory capabilities in comparison with the Soviet Union. (These are the only possibilities, unless we are prepared to risk the future on the hazard that the Soviet Empire, because of over-extension or other reasons, will spontaneously destroy itself from within.)

The argument also overlooks the imponderable, but nevertheless drastic, effects on our belief in ourselves and in our way of life of a deliberate decision to isolate ourselves. As the Soviet Union came to dominate free countries, it is clear that many Americans would feel a deep sense of responsibility and guilt for having abandoned their former friends and allies. As the Soviet Union mobilized the resources of Eurasia, increased its relative military capabilities, and heightened its threat to our security, some would be tempted to accept "peace" on its terms, while many would seek to defend the United States by creating a regimented system which would permit the assignment of a tremendous part of our resources to defense. Under such a state of affairs our national morale would be corrupted and the integrity and vitality of our system subverted.

Under this course of action, there would be no negotiation, unless on the Kremlin's terms, for we would have given up everything of importance.

It is possible that at some point in the course of isolation, many Americans would come to favor a surprise attack on the Soviet Union and the area under its control, in a desperate attempt to alter decisively the balance of power by an overwhelming blow with modern weapons of mass destruction. It appears unlikely that the Soviet Union would wait for such an attack before launching one of its own. But even if it did and even if our attack were successful, it is clear that the United States would face appalling tasks in establishing a tolerable state of order among nations after such a war and after Soviet occupation of all or most of Eurasia for some years. These tasks appear so enormous and success so unlikely that reason dictates an attempt to achieve our objectives by other means.

C. The Third Course—War.

Some Americans favor a deliberate decision to go to war against the Soviet Union in the near future. It goes without saying that the idea of "preventive" war—in the sense of a military attack not provoked by a military attack upon us or our allies—is generally unacceptable to Americans. Its supporters argue that since the Soviet Union is in fact at war with the free world now and that since the failure of the Soviet Union to use all-out military force is explainable on grounds of expediency, we are at war and should conduct ourselves accordingly. Some further argue that the free world is probably unable, except under the crisis of war, to mobilize and direct its resources to the checking and rolling back of the Kremlin's drive for world dominion. This is a powerful argument in the light of history, but the considerations against war are so compelling that the free world must demonstrate that this argument is wrong. The case for war is premised on the assumption that the United States could launch and sustain an attack of sufficient impact to gain a decisive advantage for the free world in a long war and perhaps to win an early decision.

The ability of the United States to launch effective offensive operations is now limited to attack with atomic weapons. A powerful blow could be delivered upon the Soviet Union, but it is estimated that these operations alone would not force or induce the Kremlin to capitulate and that the Kremlin would still be able to use the forces under its control to dominate most or all of Eurasia. This would probably mean a long and difficult struggle during which the free institutions of Western Europe and many freedom-loving people would be destroyed and the regenerative capacity of Western Europe dealt a crippling blow.

Apart from this, however, surprise attack upon the Soviet Union, despite the provocativeness of recent Soviet behavior, would be repugnant to many Americans. Although the American people would probably rally in support of the war effort, the shock of responsibility for a surprise attack would be morally corrosive. Many would doubt that it was a "just war" and that all reasonable possibilities for a peaceful settlement had been explored in good faith. Many more, proportionately, would hold such views in other countries, particularly in Western Europe and particularly after Soviet occupation, if only because the Soviet Union would liquidate articulate opponents. It would, therefore, be difficult after such a war to create a satisfactory international order among nations. Victory in such a war would have brought us little if at all closer to victory in the fundamental ideological conflict.

These considerations are no less weighty because they are imponderable, and they rule out an attack unless it is demonstrably in the nature of a counter-attack to a blow which is on its way or about to be delivered. (The military advantages of landing the first blow become increasingly important with modern weapons, and this is a fact which requires us to be on the alert in order to strike with our full weight as soon as we are attacked, and, if possible, before the Soviet blow is actually delivered.) If the argument of Chapter IV is accepted, it follows that there is no "easy" solution and that the only sure victory lies in the frustration of the Kremlin design by the steady development of the moral and material strength of the free world and its projection into the Soviet world in such a way as to bring about an internal change in the Soviet system.

D. The Remaining Course of Action—a Rapid Build-up of Political, Economic, and Military Strength in the Free World.

A more rapid build-up of political, economic, and military strength and thereby of confidence in the free world than is now contemplated is the only course which is consistent with progress toward achieving our fundamental purpose. The frustration of the Kremlin design requires the free world to develop a successfully functioning political and economic system and a vigorous political offensive against the Soviet Union. These, in turn, require an adequate military shield under which they can develop. It is necessary to have the military power to deter, if possible, Soviet expansion, and to defeat, if necessary, aggressive Soviet or Soviet-directed actions of a limited or total character. The potential strength of the free world is great; its ability to develop these military capabilities and its will to resist Soviet expansion will be determined by the wisdom and will with which it undertakes to meet its political and economic problems.

1. Military aspects. It has been indicated in Chapter VI that U.S. military capabilities are strategically more defensive in nature than offensive and are more potential than actual. It is evident, from an analysis of the past and of the trend of weapon development, that there is now and will be in the future no absolute defense. The history of war also indicates that a favorable decision can only be achieved through offensive action. Even a defensive strategy, if it is to be successful, calls not only for defensive forces to hold vital positions while mobilizing and preparing for the offensive, but also for offensive forces to attack the enemy and keep him off balance.

The two fundamental requirements which must be met by forces in being or readily available are support of foreign policy and protection against disaster. To meet the second requirement, the forces in being or readily available must be able, at a minimum, to perform certain basic tasks:

> a. To defend the Western Hemisphere and essential allied areas in order that their war-making capabilities can be developed;
> b. to provide and protect a mobilization base while the offensive forces required for victory are being built up;
> c. To conduct offensive operations to destroy vital elements of the Soviet war-making capacity, and to keep the enemy off balance until the full offensive strength of the United States and its allies can be brought to bear;
> d. To defend and maintain the lines of communication and base areas necessary to the execution of the above tasks; and
> e. To provide such aid to allies as is essential to the execution of their role in the above tasks.

In the broadest terms, the ability to perform these tasks requires a build-up of military strength by the United States and its allies to a point at which the combined strength will be superior for at least these tasks, both initially and throughout a war, to the forces that can be brought to bear by the Soviet Union and its satellites. In specific terms, it is not essential to match item for item with the Soviet Union, but to provide an adequate defense against air attack on the United States and Canada and an adequate defense against air and surface attack on the United Kingdom and Western Europe, Alaska, the Western Pacific, Africa, and the Near and Middle East, and on the long lines of communication to these areas. Furthermore, it is mandatory that in building up our strength, we enlarge upon our technical superiority by an accelerated exploitation of the scientific potential of the United States and our allies.

Forces of this size and character are necessary not only for protection against disaster but also to support our foreign policy. In fact, it can be argued that larger forces in being and readily available are necessary to inhibit a would-be aggressor than to provide the nucleus of strength and the mobilization base on which the tremendous forces required for victory can be built. For example, in both World Wars I and II the ultimate victors had the strength, in the end, to win though they had not had the strength in being or readily available to prevent the outbreak of war. In part, at least, this was because they had not had the military strength on which to base a strong foreign policy. At any rate, it is clear that a substantial and rapid building up of strength in the free world is necessary to support a firm policy intended to check and to roll back the Kremlin's drive for world domination.

Moreover, the United States and the other free countries do not now have the forces in being and readily available to defeat local Soviet moves with local action, but must accept reverses or make these local moves the occasion for war—for which we are not prepared. This situation makes for great uneasiness among our allies, particularly in Western Europe, for whom total war means, initially, Soviet occupation. Thus, unless our combined strength is rapidly increased, our allies will tend to become increasingly reluctant to support a firm policy on our part and increasingly anxious to seek other solutions, even though they are aware that appeasement means defeat. An important advantage in adopting the fourth course of action lies in its psychological impact—the revival of confidence and hope in the future. It is recognized, of course, that any announcement of the recommended course of action could be exploited by the Soviet Union in its peace campaign and would have adverse psychological effects in certain parts of the free world until the necessary increase in strength had been achieved. Therefore, in any announcement of policy and in the character of the measures adopted, emphasis should be given to the essentially defensive character and care should be taken to minimize, so far as possible, unfavorable domestic and foreign reactions.

2. Political and economic aspects. The immediate objectives—to the achievement of which such a build-up of strength is a necessary though not a sufficient condition—are a renewed initiative in the cold war and a situation to which the Kremlin would find it expedient to accommodate itself, first by relaxing tensions and pressures and then by gradual withdrawal. The United States cannot alone provide the resources required for such a build-up of strength. The other free countries must carry their part of the burden, but their ability and determination to do it will depend on the action the United States takes to develop its own strength and on the adequacy of its foreign political and economic policies. Improvement in political and economic conditions in the free world, as has been emphasized above, is necessary as a basis for building up the will and the means to resist and for dynamically affirming the integrity and vitality of our free and democratic way of life on which our ultimate victory depends.

At the same time, we should take dynamic steps to reduce the power and influence of the Kremlin inside the Soviet Union and other areas under its control. The objective would be the establishment of friendly regimes not under Kremlin domination. Such action is essential to engage the Kremlin's attention, keep it off balance and force an increased expenditure of Soviet resource in counteraction. In other words, it would be the current Soviet cold war technique used against the Soviet Union.

A program for rapidly building up strength and improving political and economic conditions will place heavy demands on our courage and intelligence; it will be costly; it will be dangerous. But half-measures will be more costly and more dangerous, for they will be inadequate to prevent and may actually invite war. Budgetary considerations will need to be subordinated to the stark fact that our very independence as a nation may be at stake.

A comprehensive and decisive program to win the peace and frustrate the Kremlin design should be so designed that it can be sustained for as long as necessary to achieve our national objectives. It would probably involve:

(1) The development of an adequate political and economic framework for the achievement of our long-range objectives.

(2) A substantial increase in expenditures for military purposes adequate to meet the requirements for the tasks listed in Section D-1.

(3) A substantial increase in military assistance programs, designed to foster cooperative efforts, which will adequately and efficiently meet the requirements of our allies for the tasks referred to in Section D-1-e.

(4) Some increase in economic assistance programs and recognition of the need to continue these programs until their purposes have been accomplished.

(5) A concerted attack on the problem of the United States balance of payments, along the lines already approved by the President.

(6) Development of programs designed to build and maintain confidence among other peoples in our strength and resolution, and to wage overt psychological warfare calculated to encourage mass defections from Soviet allegiance and to frustrate the Kremlin design in other ways.

(7) Intensification of affirmative and timely measures and operations by covert means in the fields of economic warfare and political and psychological warfare with a view to fomenting and supporting unrest and revolt in selected strategic satellite countries.

(8) Development of internal security and civilian defense programs.

(9) Improvement and intensification of intelligence activities.

(10) Reduction of Federal expenditures for purposes other than defense and foreign assistance, if necessary by the deferment of certain desirable programs.

(11) Increased taxes.

Essential as prerequisites to the success of this program would be (a) consultations with Congressional leaders designed to make the program the object of non-partisan legislative support, and (b) a presentation to the public of a full explanation of the facts and implications of present international trends.

The program will be costly, but it is relevant to recall the disproportion between the potential capabilities of the Soviet and non-Soviet worlds (cf. Chapters V and VI). The Soviet Union is currently devoting about 40 percent of available resources (gross national product plus reparations, equal in 1949 to about $65 billion) to military expenditures (14 percent) and to investment (26 percent), much of which is in war-supporting industries. In an emergency the Soviet Union could increase the allocation of resources to these purposes to about 50 percent, or by one-fourth.

The United States is currently devoting about 22 percent of its gross national product ($255 billion in 1949) to military expenditures (6 percent), foreign assistance (2 percent), and investment (14 percent), little of which is in war-supporting industries. (As was pointed out in Chapter V, the "fighting value" obtained per dollar of expenditure by the Soviet Union considerably exceeds that obtained by the United States, primarily because of the extremely low military and civilian living standards in the Soviet Union.) In an emergency the United States could devote upward of 50 percent of its gross national product to these purposes (as it did during the last war), an increase of several times present expenditures for direct and indirect military purposes and foreign assistance.

From the point of view of the economy as a whole, the program might not result in a real decrease in the standard of living, for the economic effects of the program might be to increase the gross national product by more than the amount being absorbed for additional military and foreign assistance purposes. One of the most significant lessons of our World War II experience was that the American economy, when it operates at a level approaching full efficiency, can provide enormous resources for purposes other than civilian consumption while simultaneously providing a high standard of living. After allowing for price changes, personal consumption expenditures rose by about one-fifth between 1939 and 1944, even though the economy had in the meantime increased the amount of resources going into Government use by $60–$65 billion (in 1939 prices).

This comparison between the potentials of the Soviet Union and the United States also holds true for the Soviet world and the free world and is of fundamental importance in considering the courses of action open to the United States.

The comparison gives renewed emphasis to the fact that the problems faced by the free countries in their efforts to build a successfully functioning system lie not so much in the field of economics as in the field of politics. The building of such a system may require more rapid progress toward the closer association of the free countries in harmony with the concept of the United Nations. It is clear that our long-range objectives require a strengthened United Nations, or a successor organization, to which the world can look for the maintenance of peace and order in a system based on freedom and justice. It also seems clear that a unifying ideal of this kind might awaken and arouse the latent spiritual energies of the free men everywhere and obtain their enthusiastic support for a positive program for peace going far beyond the frustration of the Kremlin design and opening vistas to the future that would outweigh short-run sacrifices.

The threat to the free world involved in the development of the Soviet Union's atomic and other capabilities will rise steadily and rather rapidly. For the time being, the United States possesses a marked atomic superiority over the Soviet Union which, together with the potential capabilities of the United States and other free countries in other forces and weapons, inhibits aggressive Soviet action. This provides an opportunity for the United States, in cooperation with other free countries, to launch a build-up of strength which will support a firm policy directed to the frustration of the Kremlin design. The immediate goal of our efforts to build a successfully functioning political and economic system in the free world backed by adequate military strength is to postpone and avert the disastrous situation which, in light of the Soviet Union's probable fission bomb capability and possible thermonuclear bomb capability, might arise in 1954 on a continuation of our present programs. By acting promptly and vigorously in such a way that this date is, so to speak, pushed into the future, we would permit time for the process of accommodation, withdrawal and frustration to produce the necessary changes in the Soviet system. Time is short, however, and the risks of war attendant upon a decision to build up strength will steadily increase the longer we defer it.

CONCLUSIONS AND RECOMMENDATIONS

CONCLUSIONS

The foregoing analysis indicates that the probable fission bomb capability and possible thermonuclear bomb capability of the Soviet Union have greatly intensified the Soviet threat to the security of the United States. This threat is of the same character as that described in NSC 20/4 (approved by the President on November 24, 1948) but is more immediate than had previously been estimated. In particular, the United States now faces the contingency that within the next four or five years the Soviet Union will possess the military capability of delivering a surprise atomic attack of such weight that the United States must have substantially increased general air, ground, and sea strength, atomic capabilities, and air and civilian defenses to deter war and to provide reasonable assurance, in the event of war, that it could survive the initial blow and go on to the eventual attainment of its objectives. In turn, this contingency requires the intensification of our efforts in the fields of intelligence and research and development.

Allowing for the immediacy of the danger, the following statement of Soviet threats, contained in NSC 20/4, remains valid:

"14. The gravest threat to the security of the United States within the foreseeable future stems from the hostile designs and formidable power of the U.S.S.R., and from the nature of the Soviet system.

"15. The political, economic, and psychological warfare which the U.S.S.R. is now waging has dangerous potentialities for weakening the relative world position of the United States and disrupting its traditional institutions by means short of war, unless sufficient resistance is encountered in the policies of this and other noncommunist countries.

"16. The risk of war with the U.S.S.R. is sufficient to warrant, in common prudence, timely and adequate preparation by the United States.

"*a.* Even though present estimates indicate that the Soviet leaders probably do not intend deliberate armed action involving the United States at this time, the possibility of such deliberate resort to war cannot be ruled out.

"*b.* Now and for the foreseeable future there is a continuing danger that war will arise either through Soviet miscalculation of the determination of the United States to use all the means at its command to safeguard its security, through Soviet misinterpretation of our intentions, or through U.S. miscalculation of Soviet reactions to measures which we might take.

"17. Soviet domination of the potential power of Eurasia, whether achieved by armed aggression or by political and subversive means, would be strategically and politically unacceptable to the United States.

"18. The capability of the United States either in peace or in the event of war to cope with threats to its security or to gain its objectives would be severely weakened by internal developments, important among which are:

"*a.* Serious espionage, subversion and sabotage, particularly by concerted and well-directed communist activity.

"*b.* Prolonged or exaggerated economic instability.

"*c.* Internal political and social disunity.

"*d.* Inadequate or excessive armament or foreign aid expenditures.

"*e.* An excessive or wasteful usage of our resources in time of peace.

"*f.* Lessening of U.S. prestige and influence through vacillation or appeasement or lack of skill and imagination in the conduct of its foreign policy or by shirking world responsibilities.

"*g.* Development of a false sense of security through a deceptive change in Soviet tactics."

Although such developments as those indicated in paragraph 18 above would severely weaken the capability of the United States and its allies to cope with the Soviet threat to their security, considerable progress has been made since 1948 in laying the foundation upon which adequate strength can now be rapidly built.

The Analysis also confirms that our objectives with respect to the Soviet Union, in time of peace as well as in time of war, as stated in NSC 20/4 (para. 19), are still valid, as are the aims and measures stated therein (paras. 20 and 21). Our current security programs and strategic plans are based upon these objectives, aims, and measures:

"19.

"*a.* To reduce the power and influence of the U.S.S.R. to limits which no longer constitute a threat to the peace, national independence and stability of the world family of nations.

"b. To bring about a basic change in the conduct of international relations by the government in power in Russia, to conform with the purposes and principles set forth in the U.N. Charter.

"In pursuing these objectives, due care must be taken to avoid permanently impairing our economy and the fundamental values and institutions inherent in our way of life.

"20. We should endeavor to achieve our general objectives by methods short of war through the pursuit of the following aims:

"a. To encourage and promote the gradual retraction of undue Russian power and influence from the present perimeter areas around traditional Russian boundaries and the emergence of the satellite countries as entities independent of the U.S.S.R.

"b. To encourage the development among the Russian peoples of attitudes which may help to modify current Soviet behavior and permit a revival of the national life of groups evidencing the ability and determination to achieve and maintain national independence.

"c. To eradicate the myth by which people remote from Soviet military influence are held in a position of subservience to Moscow and to cause the world at large to see and understand the true nature of the U.S.S.R. and the Soviet-directed world communist party, and to adopt a logical and realistic attitude toward them.

"d. To create situations which will compel the Soviet Government to recognize the practical undesirability of acting on the basis of its present concepts and the necessity of behaving in accordance with precepts of international conduct, as set forth in the purposes and principles of the U.N. Charter.

"21. Attainment of these aims requires that the United States:

"a. Develop a level of military readiness which can be maintained as long as necessary as a deterrent to Soviet aggression, as indispensable support to our political attitude toward the U.S.S.R., as a source of encouragement to nations resisting Soviet political aggression, and as an adequate basis for immediate military commitments and for rapid mobilization should war prove unavoidable.

"b. Assure the internal security of the United States against dangers of sabotage, subversion, and espionage.

"c. Maximize our economic potential, including the strengthening of our peacetime economy and the establishment of essential reserves readily available in the event of war.

"d. Strengthen the orientation toward the United States of the non-Soviet nations; and help such of those nations as are able and willing to make an important contribution to U.S. security, to increase their economic and political stability and their military capability.

"e. Place the maximum strain on the Soviet structure of power and particularly on the relationships between Moscow and the satellite countries.

"f. Keep the U.S. public fully informed and cognizant of the threats to our national security so that it will be prepared to support the measures which we must accordingly adopt."

. . . . .

In the light of present and prospective Soviet atomic capabilities, the action which can be taken under present programs and plans, however, becomes dangerously inadequate, in both timing and scope, to accomplish the rapid progress toward the attainment of the United States political, economic, and military objectives which is now imperative.

A continuation of present trends would result in a serious decline in the strength of the free world relative to the Soviet Union and its satellites. This unfavorable trend arises from the inadequacy of current programs and plans rather than from any error in our objectives and aims. These trends lead in the direction of isolation, not by deliberate decision but by lack of the necessary basis for a vigorous initative in the conflict with the Soviet Union.

Our position as the center of power in the free world places a heavy responsibility upon the United States for leadership. We must organize and enlist the energies and resources of the free world in a positive program for peace which will frustrate the Kremlin design for world domination by creating a situation in the free world to which the Kremlin will be compelled to adjust. Without such a cooperative effort, led by the United States, we will have to make gradual withdrawals under pressure until we discover one day that we have sacrificed positions of vital interest.

It is imperative that this trend be reversed by a much more rapid and concerted build-up of the actual strength of both the United States and the other nations of the free world. The analysis shows that this will be costly and will involve significant domestic financial and economic adjustments.

The execution of such a build-up, however, requires that the United States have an affirmative program beyond the solely defensive one of countering the threat posed by the Soviet Union. This program must light the path to peace and order among nations in a system based on freedom and justice, as contemplated in the Charter of the United Nations. Further, it must envisage the political and economic measures with which and the military shield behind which the free world can work to frustrate the Kremlin design by the strategy of the cold war; for every consideration of devotion to our fundamental values and to our national security demands that we achieve our objectives by the strategy of the cold war, building up our military strength in order that it may not have to be used. The only sure victory lies in the frustration of the Kremlin design by the steady development of the moral and material strength of the free world and its projection into the Soviet world in such a way as to bring about an internal change in the Soviet system. Such a positive program—harmonious with our fundamental national purpose and our objectives—is necessary if we are to regain and retain the initiative and to win and hold the necessary popular support and cooperation in the United States and the rest of the free world.

This program should include a plan for negotiation with the Soviet Union, developed and agreed with our allies and which is consonant with our objectives. The United States and its allies, particularly the United Kingdom and France, should always be ready to negotiate with the Soviet Union on terms consistent with our objectives. The present world situation, however, is one which militates against successful negotiations with the Kremlin—for the terms of agreements on important pending issues would reflect present realities and would therefore be unacceptable, if not disastrous, to the United States and the rest of the free world. After a decision and a start on building up the strength of the free world has been made, it might then be desirable for the United States to take an initiative in seeking negotiations in the hope that it might facilitate the process of accommodation by the Kremlin to the new situation. Failing that, the unwillingness of the Kremlin to accept equitable terms or its bad faith in observing them would assist in consolidating popular opinion in the free world in support of the measures necessary to sustain the build-up.

In summary, we must, by means of a rapid and sustained build-up of the political, economic, and military strength of the free world, and by means of an affirmative program intended to wrest the initiative from the Soviet Union, confront it with convincing evidence of the determination and ability of the free world to frustrate the Kremlin design of a world dominated by its will. Such evidence is the only means short of war which eventually may force the Kremlin to abandon its present course of action and to negotiate acceptable agreements on issues of major importance.

The whole success of the proposed program hangs ultimately on recognition by this Government, the American people, and all free peoples, that the cold war is in fact a real war in which the survival of the free world is at stake. Essential prerequisites to success are consultations with Congressional leaders designed to make the program the object of non-partisan legislative support, and a presentation to the public of a full explanation of the facts and implications of the present international situation. The prosecution of the program will require of us all the ingenuity, sacrifice, and unity demanded by the vital importance of the issue and the tenacity to persevere until our national objectives have been attained.

RECOMMENDATIONS

That the President:

a. Approve the foregoing Conclusions.

b. Direct the National Security Council, under the continuing direction of the President, and with the participation of other Departments and Agencies as appropriate, to coordinate and insure the implemention of the Conclusions herein on an urgent and continuing basis for as long as necessary to achieve our objectives. For this purpose, representatives of the member Departments and Agencies, the Joint Chiefs of Staff or their deputies, and other Departments and Agencies as required should be constituted as a revised and strengthened staff organization under the National Security Council to develop coordinated programs for consideration by the National Security Council.